UP THE CALLY

Up the Cally

The history and recollections of London's Old Caledonian Market

by

MARJORIE EDWARDS

Published by
MARKETPROMPT LIMITED
Gospel Oak Works, Oak Village
London NW5 1YA

1989

First published 1989

Copyright © 1989, Marjorie Edwards

ISBN 1 871930 00 6

Made and printed in Great Britain by

Russell Press Limited
Gamble Street, Forest Road West
Nottingham NG7 4ET

Acknowledgements

There are many wonderful old people who have happily painted a vivid picture of the past for me whilst sharing their memories over a cup of tea. There are others too, who have spent long hours corresponding with me, giving me their version of events that took place in the market.

To all those people who have contributed their stories, and to the others who have encouraged me all along the way, I dedicate this book.

Chapter One

*"They'll move Smiffield Market next and we shall lose the true
art of swearing."*

"**I** gotta horse! I gotta horse!" That was the familiar cry of Prince Monolulu, the well known racing tipster. He appeared to be about seven feet tall — a dusky Ethiopian, dressed in bright red and purple robes and crowned with a golden feathered head-dress. To a child, he was an awesome sight. Was he really a prince? Who knows? What we DO know is that he appeared regularly at the old Caledonian Market, selling his racing tips and making a few bob in the process.

He was one of the most colourful people in the market — a square mile in north-west Islington that was crammed to capacity with people and stalls, clamour and excitement, rags and riches, and in places, squalor and filth.

The hubbub started early in the morning, but at 10.00 a.m., it reached its peak. The atmosphere grew tense as the bell of the great Market Clock began to toll. Then, the gates opened and the stallholders together with their 'runners' (who were usually agile and very speedy young boys) surged through those gates like a giant tidal wave. It was everybody for himself as each one tried to grab one of the best places, and many a fight broke out over those pitches on the blue cobbled stones.

If you were around in London during the early part of this century, the chances are that this will sound very familiar. You probably went along with your parents on a Friday to see what particular bargains were on offer. Perhaps you played hookey from school and squeezed through the railings to get a glimpse of the excitement and the atmosphere that abounded there. It was pure magic — like an Aladdin's Cave.

That market was a way of life for countless thousands of London people, and today, all over the world, thousands more can recall just an occasional visit there which left them with a lasting impression. They were incredible days. Many a tale was told of a priceless treasure being picked up among the junk for a mere song.

The market touched the lives of the people who lived in the neighbouring houses of Goodinge Road, Halse Street, Corinth Road and Surr Street — names which have long since disappeared but perhaps are not yet forgotten. Market industries stretched along the length of North Road, Market Road and York Way. Four pubs stood at the corners of the market site but today, only three remain to tell the tale.

Today, a housing estate and the Caledonian Park cover the site of The Cally. The Astroturf has been built over the 'Rec' where local kids brawled and got grubby. A brand new indoor Tennis Centre will soon replace the lairs which once housed the animals while they awaited their fate.

Listen to the wind as it sighs through the trees in Caledonian Park. Can you hear the distant sound of baying animals? Look up at the turret of the Clocktower on which the golden griffin stands supreme. He could tell a tale or two of market life!

Some of the recollections in this book may stir up memories for some folk that have long since been forgotten. Close your eyes for a moment and think about those days in the Old Caledonian Market. Better still, cast your mind back a few hundred years, long before The Cally in fact . . .

*   *   *

"Well I never! I picked up one of those years ago in the Old Caledonian Market!" Did you ever hear anyone say something like that? A trite remark, but one that must have been uttered a hundred times.

Suppose you had been in London 800 years ago though, perhaps you might have heard something like this: "Tis passing strange, but I bought me just such a trinket these long years since in the Friday market at Smoothfield."

3

Eight hundred years. The history and traditions of the Old Caledonian Market at Islington go back to the days of King Henry II (1154 — 1189) for with one short break and a move of a mere mile or two, the Friday Market at "Smoothfield" and the old Caledonian Market are but one and the same thing.

The Fair of St. Bartholomew was first held at Smithfield in the reign of Henry II. Ancient records show that Rayer or Rahere, the Prior of St. Bartholomew's Priory and the founder of the present Bart's Hospital, secured a privilege from the King "To keep a fair yearly at Bartholomew tide for 3 days viz., the eve of the day, the day and the morrow with booths and standings within the church yard of the priory." It was to be held in the field of "West Smoothfield" and was at first confined to clothiers and haberdashers.

Later, King Henry granted another privilege to the citizens of London "for the standing of cattle, and stands and booths for goods, and pickage and stallage, and tolls and profits."

The Friday Pedlar's Market soon came to be an established feature of London's life in the middle ages, as a direct result of the Bartholomew Fairs. When Henry VIII proclaimed himself as the Head of the Church of England and inaugurated the Dissolution of the monasteries, the Priory of St. Bartholomew ceased to be and the privilege of the fairs were sold to Lord Rich, ancestor to the Earls of Warwick and Holland. However, the Friday Market was not to be done away with and it continued and grew in the same way — such was its popularity.

So bawdy and colourful were some of the goings-on at Smithfield, that Ben Johnson felt inspired to record them for posterity. He wrote an amusing play, "Bartholomew Fair" in 1613. Other writers too felt the need to put pen to paper in an effort to record the activities of Batholomew Fair. This anonymous poem was written in the fifteenth century:

"Here's that will challenge all the fair
Come, buy my nuts and damsons and Burgamy pears!
Here's the woman of Babylon, the Devil and the Pope
And here's a little girl, just going on the rope
Here's Dives and Lazarus, and all the world's creation
Here's the tall Dutchwoman. The like's not in the nation
Here are the booths where the high Dutch maid is
Here are the bears that dance like any ladies
Tat, tat, tat, tat, says little penny trumpet;
Here's Jacob's Hall that does so, jump it, jump it;
Sound trumpet, sound for silver spoon and fork
Come, here's your daily pig and pork."

Anon

During the early 1800's, the press was full of protests about the cruelty to cattle at Smithfield. The great increase in London's size and population also meant an increase in the number of cattle being driven into the city on market days. In wet weather, the whole area was ankle deep in mud and mire. In dry weather, myriads of flies hovered over the market and clouds of dust billowed through the surrounding streets. Traffic was held up all day long by droves of mad bullocks going to and fro and the air was rife with the cursing and swearing of the brawling drovers and dealers. There was no doubt about it. Smithfield had become a public nuisance and something had to be done. The move out of London was imminent, and unavoidable.

By 1855, the Corporation of London, in their wisdom, had sought, found and purchased a new site for the cattle market. Building had been completed and the new site was ready for occupation. Thus, they ordered the closure of Smithfield on June 11th, 1855.

What did the local residents think of this? Let's take a walk around old Smithfield with Mr. G.M. Gowan and Mr. W.S. Temple, reporters from the Illustrated London News:

THE LAST HOURS OF OLD SMITHFIELD

"On Monday 11th June, the last market was held at Smithfield. Looking from the quarter nearest to Snow Hill towards Long Lane, almost as far as the eye could see, the area was dotted with blue coats and grey, nicely yet not too strongly relieved by the brownish red of the cattle — the colour in fact, very like one of the cold coloured pictures of Teniers. The scarlet coat of the postman, hurrying through the crowd, was too powerful even for the rich deep red of the oxen to harmonise with.

"Wandering in a dreamy manner from pen to pen, the lowing and bleating might have taken us in memory to green pastures, but for the strange and strong oaths of the drovers, and the peculiar bark of the vulture-headed sheep dogs. The mind became confused with calculations as to how many millions' worth of human food had been sold? How many pounds of good English roast beef at Christmas time in the days of Good Queen Bess? How much in those of Queen Victoria? What in the interval between, and what since? How many noble men, and even women, have perished not far distant from the Priory Gate? How many witches and others? Whose ashes were they which we saw turned up a few years since on the ancient place of execution? Tournaments . . . Jousting . . .

"'Take care of your pockets, sir!' was whispered to us by a policeman. Together with the sundry hustles we have had from both animals and passengers, this served to bring us back to everyday life.

"Dogs yelped and ran over the backs of flocks of sheep. The poor animals had been standing there tied to the stake without food or water since one o'clock this morning. No use complaining to the drovers though.

"'Mind yourself mister!' grunts Mr. Drover, pushing past any lookers-on while he goes more savagely than ever bent upon his business.

"The old women who sell substantial leather and other purses, the vendors of periwinkles, whelks and such like dainties, who have from times immemorial pitched in old Smithfield, wondered — would they be allowed in the new market? The shopkeepers, with somewhat solemn faces, popped out in front and conversed gloomily together. A great deal of handshaking went on between them and well known customers.

"As the market began to clear, very small boys and some of larger growth, of the Whitechapel cut, began to disport themselves in the empty pens; Sergeant A. from a well chosen position, kept a watchful eye over the ground — notwithstanding, a great deal of pitch and toss was going on.

"Three o'clock. Still many animals left. Some of Pharoah's lean kine, and long-legged, razor-backed sheep, so thin as to be almost transparent, and which a butcher from the eastern parts pronounced to be 'rum-uns'.

"'The Last Day of the Old Market!' was the cry repeated on all sides; some obstinate individuals however, persisted that it was not the last, and bet half a sovereign to that effect.

"The faces of the drovers had, judging by the vast quantities of liquid that had been consumed in the hostelries, become more like those of the animals that they minded.

"'Goodbye old man! We shan't see you any more in the old market. Come, old fellow!' Old friends rushed into the Rose and other neighbouring inns.

"A quarter past three. The last bell of Old Smithfield was rung. Soon after, the stock on hand slowly moved off. The sweepers began to clean the ground. The six or seven banking-houses were closed, and this immense space was left in as much silence as such a place can be in this great and populous city. This, which has been a Fair and a Market for

7

more than 800 years, was closed without any ceremony — just a printed order from the Home Secretary, stuck amongst the notices on the door of the police station. And that was that."

Many a heart was heavy as the last bell tolled the closure of the old Smithfield market. Those who were closely associated with market life and depended on it for their livelihood thought that it was the end of their world. No new and modern, purpose-built live cattle market could ever take the place of something they had known all their lives, something that was dear to their very hearts.

Some of the saddest folk were the drovers who led the cows into London from the country. How did they feel? Let's ask one. His name is unknown to us, but he wore the official Drover's Badge No: 79. He wrote a lament on the last days of Smithfield — a place he had known for all of his life.

Don't speak to me Nat, I can't bear it
I'm fifty-four year old come tomorrow
And of course in my time, in this walley of tears
I've had my 'lowance of sorrow.

I've buried three wives, but that's nothink —
I mean nothink at all in comparisin' —
To the high pressure burster-of-biler-like feelings
That now is my bosom a harrassin'

To think that old Smiffield's done up!
That the days of its glory is over!
As Miss Carrolwell sings at the consart
In her beautiful song, 'The Disconsolate Drover'

Why doesn't I like the new market!
Why, Nat, bless my heart, can you ask it?
Warn't I born here in Smiffield? Or at least —
What's as good — I was left in a basket.

8

Warn't the happiest days of my life spent
In John Street and Long Lane a-goading
The bullocks as would lag behind
And make themselves so incommoding;

Or else hunting young pigs up the courts
Which there is not a doubt had misled 'em
Being much dirtier than the pigsties
Where their country sow-mothers had bred 'em.

Or twisting calves tails to make em go straight
Being a sort of boy at the weal a-steering —
(Now I don't mean that for a joke, Mister Nat,
So let's have no more of your jeering).

Or else 'prodding' the sheep which had come
Up to town for the first time that season
And whose wits had gone wool-gathering though,
I don't think sheep is actuwated by reason.

'Cos they will run a-muck. Let 'em see a cart,
Cab or coal-waggon, and under they scrambles
As though they wanted sudden death and a inquest
And not a slaughterhouse and the shambles.

I knew how 'twould be when they was about to do
Away with the fair of old Bartlemee,
And I says to a medical stud "Bartlemee's woted wulgar
So after that nothing'll startle me."

"Well" says he, "that's a blister, and was I a man
In your highly respectable station,
I'll do what Wat Tyler did years ago here in Smiffield
Pitch into the Lord Mayor and Corporation.

Why" says he, "they've done horrid things here afore
Burnt heretics when contrary!"
"Heretics?" says I. "What was they?"
"O" says he, "A breed that went out with Queen Mary"

"But what was that to bursting up Bartlemy Fair?
It's really past bearin'
They'll move Smiffield Market next
And we shall lose the true art of swearing"

And they've done it! The last market day is tomorrow,
And I can't speak for exasperation
But mark my words — we may take Sebastopol, but we've
Lost Smiffield and it's up with the British nation!

I'm a 'down pin' Nat, yes I am! When I croak
Will you go to the Ram Inn and ask Mr. Farey
If he'll let you nail up my badge in the tap room
And find room for me in his arey?

I think I might rest there, but if my ghost
Should walk it shall ask his pardon
But I've heard — THE WEDGETARIANS HAS BOUGHT
SMIFFIELD
AND INTENDS TO CONWERT IT INTO A KITCHEN
GARDEN!

Chapter Two

"Imagine a handsome country house with a red roof surrounded by wooden fencing and shady trees"

From that scene of hustle and bustle, the din, the dirt and the drovers' dealings, let's picture a more peaceful, rural setting . . .

Imagine a handsome country house with a red roof, surrounded by wooden fencing and shady trees. To the right of the house, a small archway leads to a flight of wooden stairs and an old oak door. On the opposite side is a country stile, half hidden by flowering trees, and in the front, squawking ducks and a couple of graceful swans swim lazily on a small pond, disturbing the pleasing reflection.

A rustic scene, completed by the rolling hills to the north, and green expanses to the east and west, but to the south lies the great city of gleaming spires that once caught the imagination of Dick Whittington.

It is 300 years ago now, and this is Copenhagen House — one of those questionable houses of entertainment which city dwellers visited for a day out in the country.

Copenhagen House was built by a Dane, somewhere around 1620, about the time when the King of Denmark paid a visit to his brother-in-law, James I. It certainly appears on a map of London published by Camden's Brittanica in 1695 as Coopen Hagen House.

In its heyday, the house boasted tea gardens, cricket matches, foot-racing, boxing, wrestling, pigeon-shooting and games of skittles and fives. A later landlord encouraged dog fighting and bull baiting, especially on Sunday mornings. As a consequence, his licence was revoked in 1816.

In 1780, the landlady's assistant stood at the gates and watched as a band of rioters waving blue banners and shouting loudly, approached at speed from the direction of London. So frightened was she, that she gathered her petticoats about her and scurried inside to raise the alarm.

A message was sent to Justice Hyde for a party of soldiers to protect the establishment, but as it happened, the rioters passed by. They were the Lord George Gordon rioters, on their way to Caen Wood to attack the seat of Lord Mansfield. By the time the party of soldiers arrived, the rioters were nowhere to be seen!

Soon after this false alarm, a gruesome robbery took place at the house. News of it spread far and wide, and hundreds of new visitors flocked to the scene. The crowds grew so great that additional rooms had to be built. As well as the extra rooms, a new fives court was built, and it was on this court that Cavanagh, the renowned Irish fives player won his laurels. The wall against which fives was played was the same wall that supported the kitchen chimney. When the ball resounded louder than usual, the cooks exclaimed: "Begorrah! Those are the Irishman's balls!" and the joints used to tremble on the spit.

A little later, the grounds of the house became a famous meeting place for mass political and protest meetings. on October 26th 1795, a crowd of 40,000 turned out to listen to a meeting of the London Corresponding Society who sympathised with the French Revolution. These meetings gave the government cause for alarm and four members of the Society were tried for treason.

In 1812, a grand proposal was put forward to bring sea water in from Essex by means of great iron pipes in order to make an open air bathing pool for Londoners, but the whole scheme proved to be far too costly.

On 21st April 1834 a great meeting of trade union members gathered together in the Fields to start a procession to London. They had a petition of some 260,000 names protesting against the savage sentences passed against their colleagues, the Tolpuddle Martyrs (also known as the Dorchester Labourers). Today, a sycamore tree, planted by Ray Buckton of the N.U.R in April 1984 marks the site.

But Copenhagen House and Fields had outlived its day and its usefulness by 1852. Mr. Batson, the freeholder of the 70 acres of land around the House decided to sell. He knew that the Corporation of London were looking for a new site for the live cattle market which was becoming a nuisance at Smithfield. He instructed his solicitor, Mr. Lee, to meet with Mr. Bunning, the City Architect and to offer his land to the Corporation for the sum of £400,000. The deeds were signed on 13th May 1852, and with Mr. Batson's signature, the death warrant for Copenhagen House was signed.

From that moment on, the grassy site became a hive of activity. Plans were drawn, rejected, re-drawn, altered and finally, approved, and Mr. J.B. Bunning, the City Architect, was heard to complain that 'he was tired of drawing such an amazing number of plans!'

Firstly, the thirty acre site was laid out in a neat square of Staffordshire blue bricks which were supplied by Messrs James Wood and Son from their works at Portway, near Oldbury, Birmingham. More than three million bricks were used on the building site.

Two broad cross roads traversed the square so that all roads led to the central focal point — Bank Buildings, a twelve sided polygon which was the nucleus and centre for all the commerce of the market.

Bank Buildings contained six banks, the offices of the three major railway companies, the Electric International Telegraph Company, and the office of the Clerk of the Market. There was also a drover's resting and reading room and a store which sold anything and everything for the comfort of the animals, including horse-rugs, loin cloths, stable blankets, boots and boot-hose, sacks and nosebags and all kinds of horse-balls, cattle-drenches and animal medicines.

One of the first banking firms to occupy numbers 5, 7 and 9 Bank Buildings was Messrs W. and J. Biggerstaff. These bankers had moved to the market from Smithfield, where they had operated a banking service for the traders in the live cattle market. In later years, these bankers were swallowed up by the National Provincial Bank which in turn went on to become the National Westminster. The Midland Bank also had offices in Bank Buildings, although not right from the beginning since the Midland did not move to London from Birmingham until 1891. Another smaller bankers, Hill and Co., rented an office in Bank Buildings right from the market's opening days.

The London and North Western Railway Company had an office in the market. In 1855, this line was responsible for bringing in 70,000 oxen and 240,000 sheep. The Great Northern Line brought in a further 15,000 oxen and 120,000 sheep, but by far the most important line for transporting the animals was the Eastern Counties Railway. This line crossed through the rich feeding counties of Essex, Cambridgeshire and Norfolk, and brought in 81,000 head of oxen and 270,000 sheep.

The Electric International Telegraph Company, founded by Sir William Fothergill Cook and Joseph Lewis Ricardo in 1846, had an office at Bank Buildings in connection with their agreement to construct and maintain telegraphs for the railway companies. It was through this office that messages were received from all parts of the country concerning cattle movements. A forerunner of British Telecom, this office in the market provided a useful service.

The Clerk of the Market was responsible for the general day to day running of business. He was there to be consulted in cases of enquiry or to arbitrate when a scuffle broke out. He also posted up on a notice board the expected daily arrival of cattle and sheep, once a telegraph message had been received.

One of his other duties was to keep a Complaints Book and many and varied are some of the complaints that he received:

On August 22nd 1864, Mr. George Currier of 17 Camden Road Villas had a few choice words to say about the nuisance of dogs in the market. He complained that they were worrying the sheep and making too much noise.

James Wheatley, a lamplighter, is recorded as being cautioned several times for carelessness in his duties and for neglecting to turn out the gas at the proper times.

In August 1864 and again in May 1865, John Layton, Clerk of the Vestry of the Parish of St. Mary's complained that stagnant blood, water and manure were allowed to accumulate in the rear of Balmoral Grove causing 'an abominable stench'!

Many and frequent were the complaints of salesmen on being moved from their regular pitches, but after 1865, no more complaints were recorded. Maybe with the increasing size and use of the market, there were too many to bother with!

While the Clerk of the Market presided over his domain from the ground, the soaring turret of the Market Clock was lord of all it surveyed. Standing 160 feet high, it was, and still is, one of the largest turret clocks in London. It could be seen for many miles around, and is still a renowned Islington landmark. In its construction, 880 square feet of glass were used; the main wheels were 3 feet across and it had a winding weight of 7 cwt. The Leisure Hour Magazine of 1855 described it as "a graceful novelty in commercial architecture." Its bell chimed every 15 minutes and at the very top, a gilded griffin weather vane, the size of a small pony, glistened in the sunlight.

On the blue cobbled stones, 13,000 feet of rail were constructed which could accommodate 6000 beasts. A further 1800 pens housed 35,000 sheep. The whole of the market square was surrounded by iron pillars sunk deep into the ground and painted red. Mr. J. Bell designed the carved animals heads — a lamb, a cow, a horse and a pig together with a coat of arms, which adorned each pillar in turn.

On the opposite side of Market Road were the animal lairs, comfortably fitted up for the reception and housing of the livestock while they waited for market day. The lairs were provided with plenty of straw, food and water to ensure the comfort of the animals. A fountain stood at the entrance to the lairs, and many a tale is told of cows running straight into the fountain after their long and tiring journey from the country!

On the northern edge of the market, The Queens Hotel and The City Hotel stood side by side to welcome the enormous influx of visitors which were now expected in this corner of Islington, but alas, their life as hotels was not very long. After twenty years or so, they became the Queens Arms Buildings and the City Arms Buildings, and finally in 1915, Queens Mansions and City Mansions, providing much needed housing for the area.

Between these two large blocks, The Drovers Hall and Asylum was built in 1873. It consisted of 15 flats of three rooms, built on two floors, for 15 aged and infirm drovers. There was also a committee room with offices and a large hall for use as a club room by the drovers working in the markets. Mention of the Drovers Hall is made in the Illustrated London News of August 9, 1873:

"A raised dais at one end of this magnificently decorated hall will afford an opportunity for the delivering of lectures and other means of improving the minds of this class of our fellow-countrymen who need it not a little!"

The public houses which stood at the four corners of the market site — The Lamb, The Lion, The White Horse and The Black Bull, took over what hotel trade there was to be had, and at the same time, provided an ample means of refreshment for the market workers. They opened at four in the morning to cater for the drovers' liquid breakfasts and closed at five in the evening, when trade was drawing to a close, and folk were having 'one last drink for the road'.

The whole of the new Metropolitan Cattle Market at Copenhagen Fields was superb in its design, planned and laid out with as much thought for the comfort of the animals as for the people who were involved in the trade — those who drove the animals, those who bartered for them and those who slaughtered them.

Chapter Three

*"The proceedings of this day are of deep interest and importance
to the great community of the metropolis"*

On Wednesday 13th June 1855, 47 grand carriages arrived in an imposing cortège, ready for the grand state opening of the Metropolitan Cattle Market. The Lord Mayor and the Corporation were ready to welcome HRH Prince Albert who was well known for his interest in agriculture, and indeed, who had won prizes himself for cattle breeding, and notably, the First Prize in the Paris Exhibition.

They all proceeded slowly around the market to loud cheers from the well dressed crowd of important people who filled the vast concourse.

After inspecting as much as he could in the time allowed, the Prince and his entourage entered the spacious marquee which had been erected on the site by Mr. Benjamin Edgington. The marquee was capable of accommodating 1700 people and it was decorated tastefully in a manner which befitted such a great occasion:

"Amongst the decorations were the medallions which adorned the Guildhall on the occasion of the Emperor's visit, and in addition, fanciful designs of ploughs, sickles, scythes and other agricultural implements. The armorial bearings of the great grazing counties were prominently displayed, as also those of the foreign countries from which of late years we have, thanks to Free-trade, drawn such abundant supplies of cattle; and within the tent, the various supporting poles were decorated with trophies in which the Union Jack and the friendly Tricolor were tastefully intermingled."

(From the Illustrated London News, 15th June 1855)

In the marquee, the Prince stood in front of the magnificent state chair which had been brought specially from the Guildhall for the occasion. The Lord Mayor's Recorder read out the following address to His Majesty:

"May it please your Royal Highness that we, her Majesty's dutiful and loyal subjects, the Lord Mayor, Aldermen and Commons of the City of London, desire by the warmest expression of our gratitude to testify to your Royal highness the value which we attribute to your gracious presence on this occasion.

"The proceedings of this day are of deep interest and importance to the great community of the metropolis and to the country at large. These costly and extensive works have been undertaken by the Corporation of the City of London in deference to the suggestions of the national legislature.

"If the transfer of the chief Metropolitan Market to this new and spacious locality shall be successful, it will not only have removed all ground of complaint arising from the character of its ancient site, but will also have conferred essential benefits upon the population of this vast capital as well as on those important branches of our national industry which are concerned in supplying with food the increasing masses of its inhabitants and the countless numbers who frequent it.

"In the happiness and prosperity of all classes of her Majesty's subjects, your Royal Highness has always evinced the warmest and most active interest and we know nothing more likely to secure success to this great undertaking than the sanction and encouragement afforded in its inauguration by the illustrious consort of the Queen."

In his reply, Prince Albert thanked the Lord Mayor and Corporation for his warm welcome and said that he was much pleased by the kind invitation to admire the great new work, and that he was sure that it would be eminently conducive to the comfort and health of the City of London.

He went on to say that although the farmers and the traders may have been saddened by the closure of Smithfield, they would no doubt soon appreciate the boon conferred on them by the Corporation of London, for all the new facilities and amenities now offered to them.

Amongst the guests, many well known and well-to-do names from society and politics rubbed shoulders with the Mayors from several important provincial towns, and while the massed bands from the Caledonian and Chelsea Asylums and the Foundling Hospital provided the music, the whole company sat down to a splendid and elegant repast provided by Messrs. Staples from the Albion.

The Lord Mayor's chaplain, Rev. F. Moon, said the grace and then there followed a number of toasts to the health and success of everybody and everything.

Late in the afternoon, the whole company departed, after a grand time being had by all. The new Metropolitan Cattle Market was now officially open and raring to go for business on Friday 15th June.

After its grand spread covering the Inauguration of the new market, the Illustrated London News devoted a small paragraph to the first day of its trading:

"A fine herd of bullocks consigned to Mr. Neve, salesman of Norfolk, was the first that entered the Cattle-Market and it was not long until part was purchased by Mr. William Bee of Newgate Market and paid for to the bankers, Messrs. Hill and Sons.

"One fine bullock was taken to the public slaughter-houses and slaughtered by Mr. W.T. Farey of the Ram, Smithfield, so that this bullock may be said to have been the first entered for sale, the first sold, the first bought, the first paid for, the first delivered, the first removed and the first slaughtered in the New Market!

"A little before noon, cows were entered at the north-east corner of the market allotted for them, and sales were immediately commenced. At 2 pm the horse market commenced at the opposite south eastern corner.

"The concourse of butchers carts was immense so that the relief in the neighbourhood of Smithfield must have already been great.

"For Friday, the market lairs were not very liberally patronised, but on the evening of that day, some fine lots arrived from the north for the Monday market, while fresh arrivals swelled the number by almost every train on Saturday, so that considering the change of the market site and the season of the year and the want of experience, the Corporation, we presume, are satisfied with this part of the experiment.

"Altogether, the trade have expressed themselves very favourably towards the first day of the new market."

Thus, the new Metropolitan Cattle Market had arrived in Islington, and looked all set to do business for many years to come.

Chapter Four

The morning is clear and bright, bathed in a grey mist of steam, spouting from the nostrils of thousands of cattle and sheep.

Can you imagine what it must have been like in those early days at the New Cattle Market?

Let us suppose we set off early one morning, perhaps in the 1870's, to go and see a great cattle show. It has been a frosty week and a rapid thaw has set in now. As a result, the roads around the market are one dismal swamp of mud, blocked with butchers gigs, traps, and carts, and crowds of people are tramping through this mire, ankle deep towards the scene of the action.

The morning is clear and bright but the whole area is bathed in a grey mist of steam, spouting from the nostrils of thousands of cattle and tens of thousands of sheep. They stand in crowded ranks, awaiting the decree which consigns them to their fate.

The air is rife with pungent animal smells. Bulls are bellowing, sheep are bleating and dogs are barking vociferously to create one unholy din.

Most of the salesman have not yet put in an appearance. The old habit of doing business at daybreak which was so characteristic of Smithfield, is slowly dying out, for with the increased conveniences that the new market offers, there is not the same necessity for rising at dawn.

A huge oxen is paraded in front of the buyers. He threads his way through the narrow alleys, being punched on the quarter and tickled on the flank. Two men shake hands, then out come the long bladed scissors and the buyer cuts his mark on the hide. The first sale of the day is made, amidst a raucous din of animal grunts and drovers' yells.

In this corner of London, you can meet all manner of folk from every county between South Wales and Northumberland, or even farther north. Listen carefully and you can hear as many dialects as there are English towns! The stubby round-faced Welshman stares up at his huge Scottish cousin, standing six foot three in his shoes and measuring almost as much in diameter! Here is the breeder from the fens, a good twelve inches taller than the London drover, and wrapped in leather from his heels to his waist.

A wizened old man, his lips half hidden by a moustache demands, "Which is moy woy till 'Oigate?"

Young girls, barefooted and beshawled, hover around the animal pens without a thought of fear. Rather, they are more interested in attracting the attentions of some handsome young salesman or the eye of a stalwart drover. Scruffy kids carrying chipped earthenware jugs, run to and from the lairs, sent on an errand to fetch a penn'orth of fresh milk for mother.

Meanwhile, the morning wanes. A watery sun gives a hint of warmth, and business grows brisker. Buyers are arriving thick and fast and the hotel yards are full of their gigs and carts. A hundred London butchers, complete with their professional blue frocks, invade the scene.

A sheep-owner who has been waiting for the butchers to arrive for the last four hours, cannot wait any longer for his breakfast. He dares not leave the sheep in case he misses a sale, so he eats at his post, plate balanced precariously while he attempts to carve his rasher of ham, eat his buttered toast and wash it down with a mug of steaming coffee, all at one and the same time

There is a dense crowd around the Polygon and Tower. Boys are hawking ground-ash sticks, peppermint, toffee and brandy balls while others are handing out shopkeeper's bills.

Dogs are tethered to the rails in the calf-shed, some of them so exhausted by their long journeys of the last few days and nights, that they scarcely have the power to move. The older dogs have the sense to conserve their remaining strength and to stretch themselves out and sleep, while the young ones, even though exhausted with weariness, bark furiously at the passing droves of sheep.

The whole place is a hive of activity. There is plenty to see and plenty going on throughout the day, until the dusk begins to fall. Little by little, the hue and cry dies down. Animals are led away, people go off to their homes and a silver moon casts an eerie glow over the empty pens. The market clock strikes sonorously, and, as if on cue, the intermittent lowing of the cattle in the lairs breaks the silence of the evening. Another day at the Cattle Market is over.

*   *   *

The moving of the cattle market from Smithfield to this corner of Islington was undoubtedly a success for the meat trade. The cattle were arriving at the lairs in great numbers; they were housed comfortably until the appropriate market days when a display of frenzied activity broke out. They were sold and either slaughtered on the spot, or driven away with their new butcher owners, and then silence ensued again until the next market day.

Houses, trades and industries were growing up fast in the newly built streets all around the market site and in just over a year since it had opened, the cattle market was a bustling, thriving activity at the centre of a newly developing industrial community.

But what of the old Smithfield pedlars who had traded beside the empty cattle pens from time immemorial?

For a while it appeared as if the centuries old "Friday market" had come to a painful end for them, for no provision had been made for the pedlars on the new site at Islington. Some of them sought for themselves a stall at one of the other London street markets, while others suffered severe hardship and fell into distressed circumstances.

But costers are not the sort to suffer such an injustice without a fight. They organised repeated protests on their own behalf until finally, permission was granted to re-open the Friday Market at Copenhagen Fields "according to ancient custom, among the empty cattle pens," and so, the costermongers of old London came to claim for themselves "a pitch on the stones" with the market whose fortunes they and their ancestors had shared for the last 700 years.

The new market though, was not quite the same as being at Smithfield. A few years had passed in between, and the tradition had been broken. People were not used to going out to Islington to buy the goods which they had sought at Smithfield on a Friday. The age-old popularity of Friday Market had temporarily disappeared . . .

With any people less persistent and enterprising than the Cockney costers, it might have disappeared forever, but to a Cockney, old traditions die hard. Gradually, these people built up for themselves a new 'Smithfield' and it wasn't too long before the word began to spread that bargains were to be found at the new cattle market in Islington . . .

Little by little, the trickle of people from London grew into a crowd. The crowds returned home with their purchases, and told their friends. The friends went along to see what they too could find in the market, and before very long, the numbers of visitors grew in size, so that by the turn of the century, Friday Market, in all its glory and confusion was back — but this time, it was far bigger and better than anything Smithfield had ever seen!

The well known writer and essayist, J.B. Priestley, like many of his contemporaries, often visited the market, and in one of his essays, written in 1932, he describes a typical day, and the traders, typical of the Caledonian Market for us:

"On most days, this open market off the Caledonian Road is very open and very Caledonian, so grey and bleak that you might be bargaining on the summit of the Cairngorms. That it is possible to do a brisk trade in ice-cream and glasses of sea-green lemonade on that windy height only proves that man is a romantic and imaginative creature. Indeed, the whole Caledonian Market proves that.

"Consider the American visitors, who may be seen any Friday, looking a little pinched, at the stalls where jewelled brooches and silver dishes, amber and ivories are offered for sale. The people who own these stalls are either dark-skinned young men or fat, needle-eyed women, and a glance at them tells you that they would rather die than sell a thing for less than one hundred and fifty per cent profit. But these visitors from America, the place where all good legends go to when they die, see these brooches and ivories against the grey Caledonian background, and so imagine there are tremendous bargains to hand. And so there are. You may pay ten shillings more for a silver bowl or an amber necklace in the Caledonian Market than you would pay in a decent shop in the centre of the city, but you are being given more than ten shillings' worth of romantic legend with the articles. The story of how you picked them up will be worth a whole heap of dollars to you, once back in the home town.

"This is a trivial example, however, and does not touch the market proper, which these artful merchants of jewellery have no right to attend. Wander down those long aisles there into which the oldest lumber-rooms — nay, the very dustbins seem to have been emptied — and then you can begin to understand how this one surviving pedlar's market or rag-fair fosters the kindliest romantic illusions.

"It does this by patching together every Tuesday and Friday, the last shreds of self respect in broken men. You are, we will say, nearly sixty years of age and in a wretched state of health. It is ten years since you were sacked from your last little regular job. You have a bent back, flat feet, no teeth, a wheezing voice, and you cannot even shave yourself. If your son (who drives a bus) and your brother (who still keeps the fried fish shop in Hoxton) did not slip you anything, and your daughter occasionally share her dole with you, no doubt you could not exist outside the workhouse.

"Nevertheless, you are no mere beggar, even if things are not always going too well. As a matter of fact, you have a little business of your own. You are in the second-hand, the buying and selling line. You are a trader in the Caledonian Market. Out of your dilapidated suitcase, you produce certain articles — perhaps a dirt cushion, two egg cups, an under-skirt, the "Letters of Charles Kingsley", and a broken alarm-clock, and these you offer to the public. There you stand from ten to four, exchanging remarks about the weather and the state of trade with your fellow merchants, and even though nobody ever buys anything from you, the fact remains that you are in business, just as Dick Whittington was and Mr. Selfridge is. Every Friday, dignity returns to you."

From "Self-Selected Essays" by J.B. Priestley, 1932. Reprinted by permission of William Heinemann Ltd.

The feeling and atmosphere of market days are well and truly captured in his essay. The Caledonian Market — it was a place that somehow endeared itself to many a heart, and when it had, it earned itself the affectionate nickname of "The Cally".

The buyers who went there at first were mostly poorer people in search of second hand clothes and cheap food so the pedlars searched high and low for articles hitherto thrown on to the scrapheaps. Goods had to be bought for next to nothing and the search for them wasn't just confined to London. The pedlars went further and further afield to find their goods, and soon they became quite familiar figures around the countryside, in their donkey carts, going "totting".

The contents of dusty lumber rooms in farm houses and country mansions could be bought up for a few pence and the householders were glad to be rid of all their accumulated 'rubbish'. It was these contents of dusty lumber rooms and old English country houses which earned for the Cally its international reputation, for the pedlars did not realise the richness and scarcity of their wares —

Not until one fine day when a virtuoso, skilled in the art and knowledge of beautiful and ancient ornaments found himself with nothing better to do, so he wandered off the beaten track — and into The Cally. Amongst the pile of second hand clothes and bric a brac thrown about the stones, he found such an astounding bargain, that he could hardly believe his luck. He hurried away and boasted about it to his friends. Thereafter, a very different class of buyer came along to inspect the wares amongst the heaps of 'rubbish', and The Cally

became the strangest meeting place of east and west in the whole of London.

Fur-wrapped society women stepped from expensive carriages to mingle in the crowd with shawl-covered, bare-footed housewives. Connoisseurs of art and beauty came to hunt for Rembrandts and haggled across the width of a barrow with a cloth capped coster.

Much to the annoyance and envy of the established antique dealers of the West End, who had spent years accumulating their knowledge, The Cally was fast becoming known as THE place in London to buy antiques. The American tourists in London were flocking to the Cally in droves. Film stars and actors alike hovered over the stalls and fought over anything out of the ordinary, and to own something precious and be able to say 'I picked it up at The Cally' became all the rage!

The clamour and the din provided a rakish atmosphere which was a veritable melting pot of glamour and squalor, riches and rags, excitement and glorious confusion. No wonder it was irresistible to the thousands upon thousands who regularly went up The Cally to spend the whole day there, sorting through the pedlars wares, furnishing their homes, seeking new clothes or buying provisions. Or merely idling away their time.

Idling away the time was never difficult for in its heyday, The Cally boasted more than 2000 stalls, all tightly crammed into the market square with never an inch to spare. A day was never long enough to see all that there was to be seen; to stop and listen to the endless patter of the con men, to laugh at some of the costers' crude jokes, or to pause awhile with a tuppeny bowl of jellied eels, some hot apple fritters, or a stick of hokey pokey and watch yet another brawl break out!

To spend a day at The Cally was like spending a day in another world — a friendly, warm, intimate world of fun and laughter and jostling crowds. The Cally was all things to all people. To kids, it was Paradise — earning a penny here and a ha'penny there and scavenging among the left-overs; to mums and dads, it was the greatest shopping centre around, and to Walter Sickert, the renowned artist who lived in Islington in 1934, it was his idea of heaven.

Chapter Five

"No place can be more depressing on a day of pouring rain when the need to make some cash is urgent . . ."

It wasn't always heaven for the stall-holders though. They had their good days and they had their bad ones too. There were days when they arrived in grand spirits with plenty of good, new stock to sell and fully expecting to make a killing. Then there were the days when they arrived at the besieged market gates with precious little on their carts and wondering why they had even bothered to come at all. One could never tell what a day would bring.

Jane Brown was a stall-holder at the Cally in the nineteen-thirties. She didn't come from a family of traders — in fact, quite the opposite. Her parents were wealthy people and her father had made a tidy sum on the Stock Exchange. Together, her parents had had great expectations for their youngest daughter's future, but as a rebellious teenager, she met a certain young man by name of Don . . . and fell in love! It wasn't long before Don and Jane set up home in Hampstead, but in the depressing years following the First World War, they both found it difficult to get jobs, until one day, when they were at an all time low, a friend told them about the Caledonian Market . . .

The young couple decided to try their luck on a hot sunny day in June, 1919, taking with them anything and everything they could lay their hands on. They hired a van and drove to the market, along with the usual motley collection of motors and horse-drawn carriages and anything else on wheels that remotely resembled a vehicle, and they waited in the queue with a thousand others for the ten o'clock "mad rush".

By three o'clock on their first day, Don and Jane had sold out of everything and made the grand total of forty pounds. They were rich! But what's more — they were hooked on being marketeers! From that moment on, they scarcely looked back.

Don and Jane spent fourteen years "on the stones" at The Cally, although in actual fact, Jane spent much of that time selling alone, due to Don's constant ill health. She grew to love the community of men and women who earned their living there. She found the atmosphere alive and vital. She recognised the courage, the character and the camaraderie of her fellow stall-holders, so much so, that when the market closed in August 1939, it was she who led the Caledonian Market Trader's Association in their campaign to get the market re-opened.

Jane kept a diary of her life in the market and eventually had it published in book form. She called it "I had a Pitch on the Stones" and in it, she summed up her fascination for the place and the way of life she loved:

"It is difficult to know why The Stones should fascinate me so. No place can be more tiring on a hot summer day, with great crowds shuffling to and fro past the pitches, all too few of them out to buy, and all too many of them examining this and that, asking questions, and trying to give the impression that they would buy, but only the thing is . . . well, it's not quite . . . you know . . .

"No place can be more depressing on a day of pouring rain when the need to make some cash is urgent, but the probability of doing so is as remote as the moon.

"Certainly, no place in London can be more like the Arctic in mid-winter with a north-east wind cutting across like an icy blade and darting in amongst the covered stalls in gusts that go right through you. On days like that, people keep their hands in their pockets and their money stays in there too.

"No place can be more exasperating. It might have been a fair day one Friday, but with nothing very special in the way of goods to sell. The next Friday, it's a day full of fine anticipations. You arrive at the market with a stock that you're sure is going to sell like hot cakes. The weather is good; the crowds are out in force. A few minor sales are made quite quickly and there is no doubt that the day ahead is going to be one of the best yet. But — nothing of the kind. Two or three big sales almost come off — but not quite. Then a few trifles go, but after that, the hours drag and you take nothing. At the end of the day, you have come near to setting up a new all-time low, and you pack up and go home, puzzled, tired and dispirited. Yet the same goods that hung around so badly that day might go like wildfire the next week.

"That's just one side of the picture, though. There are days when it is a delight to stand there. All the customers seem especially friendly and you can talk brightly with no effort at all. Whether you sell anything or not doesn't seem to matter (although it does really, of course).

"Sometimes there are days when there are pleasant surprises — something that seemed a doubtful piece finds a quick buyer at a good price. Perhaps the weather, which had been so ominous and overcast on leaving home, clears up, and bright warm sunshine welcomes a good throng of shoppers. Maybe you'll be polishing up an ornament ready for putting on show when suddenly, it turns out to be more valuable than you had originally thought . . .

"Perhaps that's where some of the fascination lies. It is all so incalculable."

It wasn't just Jane Brown who was fascinated by The Stones. Thousands of stall-holders, shoppers, visitors and tourists alike took The Cally to their hearts, not only for the weekly shopping or the hunt for bargains among the junk but also for the 'street theatre' that plied its trade in and amongst the stalls. Indeed, some of those actually selling their wares had such a line in patter that they could have held their own up on the stage next to any well-known actor!

Perhaps the Nottingham Mystery Man was best known. He wore a mask over his face from chin to brow and from the moment his huge van arrived, the crowds would jostle for a place. He began by selling his parcels of sweets by Dutch auction. He started at four pounds and worked his way down, filling in with jokes on the way.

There was a method in his madness. The customers bought his mystery parcels for half a crown, never mind that there was only a few penn'orth of sweets inside. Occasionally, there would be a complaint. "Ladies and Gentlemen," said the Mystery Man. "Listen to this. I want you to know that there's been a complaint. A customer of mine is complaining, but my customers must NOT complain. I forbid it by law! Everybody must be satisfied with what they've bought. Now Madam," (addressed to the lady who made the complaint.)

"Now, madam. I see you are dissatisfied, but not for long. Here is a parcel for you, and you personally. If I auction it, I may get five shillings (25p) or I may get five pounds. Who knows? You don't know and I don't know. None of us knows. It's a mystery. Life is a mystery and I'm the Mystery Man! Here is your parcel, Madam. There's no auction now, no price to pay. This parcel is for you. It's a present. It's free. Gratis. I give it to you for nothing. Accept it with my compliments!"

At the end of his auction, the Mystery Man remained a mystery. He put everything away, closed his van and with his mask still in place, he drove away.

Mad Jack was another one who drew crowds like a magnet to his furniture stall. Poor old Jack really was touched in the head and his predicament became ten times worse after a liquid dinner! Feeling more than a little inebriated, Mad Jack would hold up an ornamental china vase and get carried away into a frenzy of salesmanship. "What about this one?" he would bellow at the top of his voice. "Yer auntie Maud's precious china vase. Who wants the f---ing thing? How much will you give me for the b------?"

Before anyone had a chance to reply, Jack would hurl it to the ground where it fell in a shower of smitherines. "Well you can't f---ing 'ave it now, can you!" Mad Jack would shout triumphantly, and then leap onto the next object — a chest of drawers. A few hefty kicks, and that was beyond repair, then Jack would jump on it, and finish it off to a pile of firewood. "That's that then!" Said Jack, and he'd fall amongst the ruins of his stall in an exhausted untidy heap!

What an assortment of nicknames those stall holders earned for themselves!

Doc Warren was a short, thick-set little fellow with a head that was slightly too large for his body. He sold pills that would "make a man of you." Like Mad Jack, Doc fared better with a pint or two of "wallop" inside him! When he got going, Doc would really go to town with his patter: "Call yourselves men, all of you? Why, some of you don't even know what it is to sit down for a hearty meal with a hearty appetite. Now you lot just take a look at me, because I'm as 'ealthy as 'ealthy can be. I eat like a pig; I sleep like a pig and I drink like a pig . . ."

"Yes mate, and you look like a blinkin' pig!" Shouts a voice from the back of the crowd. The audience roars with laughter, and moves on for the next live show. Poor Doc didn't sell any more of his amazing pills for an hour or two after that, but he did earn himself a new nickname — that of Piggy Warren, a name which stuck with him for the rest of his life.

The Banana King, needless to say, never did anything but a roaring trade. Perhaps that's how he came by his name! His huge van was piled high with great hands of bananas which he practically gave away . . . even a giant bunch, almost too big to carry, could be had for less than one and sixpence! He didn't need to attract a crowd, but invariably, his audience would surround the van. He held their attention by rapidly breaking up a hand of bananas and throwing them into the crowds, one by one. "'Ere you are, mother! A banana for you, and one for you too, missus!"

If the banana king treated his wares a trifle unceremoniously, another of the fruit merchants, a real gentleman in his Antony

40

Eden hat, more than made up for that. His stall was packed to capacity with every kind of exotic fruit imaginable. His manner, in keeping with his dress, was calm and serene, and his voice described in dulcet tones, the rare excellence of the produce he was selling for a mere two shillings a bag. Whisking a silken kerchief from his well-groomed jacket pocket, he would gaze at each orange with loving pride before flicking off the imaginary dust and lowering it reverently into the roomy brown bag.

"Peaches like a maiden's cheek," his voice caressed the words as he gracefully placed the fruit beside the nearest rosy cheek to him. The ladies loved it all. Black grapes or ripe strawberries? This artist had them all, and each satisfied housewife went away with a bag full of fruit, feeling like a duchess on the receiving end of his undivided attention.

Fishy Bill and his wife presided over their stall loaded high with denizens from the vasty deep. The couple themselves were of as much interest to the onlookers as the wares they sold, for their surname was Dove, yet two creatures more un-dovelike would have been difficult to find — they fought like cat and dog! Great lorries from the north carried Fishy Bill's marine creatures to market where they rested on giant slabs of ice, waiting to struggle with their purchasers and be tamed before being carted off home and fed to a hungry family.

Large whole salmon with beady eyes, crusty cray fish, unwieldy lobsters with sinister claws, shiny herrings and soft roes — fresh and fearsome, horned and ugly, they were all auctioned off quickly and no reasonable offer was ever refused. Wrapped up inadequately in newspapers, some of these creatures even looked like old Bill himself with their wet whiskers hanging morosely at the side of their faces!

Charlie Boy was a dapper fellow, a handsome bell-boy, six feet tall . . . and made entirely of plywood! His owner was of much smaller stature and sold American oilcloth. Perhaps his diminished height gave him a minor complex, for he never addressed the crowds while he spoke. He kept his eyes resolutely fixed on his model whilst spreading out each bright piece of cloth before Charlie Boy's very eyes and treating him to a lavish description of the mouth-watering meals that could be spread before him on such cloth. These tactics soon disposed of his wares. Only when a cloth was sold would Charlie Boy's owner enter into any conversation with his clients, then along with their purchase, he would sell them a cautionary tale!

Then there were others who by virtue of their looks or the product they sold, will forever be remembered by a nickname. Mr. Kolene sold toilet goods — soaps, talc, perfumes and powder, along with hair potions and incredible shampoos. Brilliantine was all the rage amongst the men, but for those whose hair was beginning to thin out a little, there was "Kolene" — a fantastic, miracle-working cure for baldness. Oddly enough, Mr. Kolene was bald himself!

"Get yer 'air cut, Mr. Kolene!" was a familiar shout at his stall.

Some folk were suckers for some of the so-called 'miracle cures' sold by the 'quack' doctors. One Eyed Harry, in black top hat and tails with a black patch over one eye, sold Rowlands and Paragoric lozenges for coughs and colds. Doubtless he did a good trade — especially in the winter months when wind and rain whipped across The Stones. Frequently, his own voice would suffer from his non-stop sales patter. "'Ave a couple o' Rowlands, 'Arry! That should 'elp a bit!" folk were quick to cry.

Of all the quack doctors with their miracle cures, Charlie wins the prize hands down for being the funniest. Charlie was a herbalist, selling a remedy which he called 'God's own gift to man'. Beer to Charlie wasn't just a drink — it was his life's study. He knew everything there was to know about beer. He had sampled and criticised every known brand, and before he even started his day's work, Charlie had to sample a good half dozen pints or else he couldn't "put any steam into it!"

One day, poor old Charlie was down on his luck. It was the middle of winter and he had no money and nothing to sell either, nevertheless, he turned up at the market gates sharp at ten o'clock and grabbed his usual pitch.

"I hadn't got a clue what I was going to do," says Charlie, "so I went to a fruit stall and begged myself an empty orange box, when what did I see, but a huge banana stalk what had been throwed away. All of a sudden likes, the idea struck me!"

Charlie took his penknife and cut up the banana stalk into neat little pieces and arranged them on to the upturned box. Next, he removed a shoe and a sock. "There was nuffink else for it. I can't figure out why a bloke with a bare foot attracts a crowd, but he always does, sure as eggs is eggs! There's summat about a foot what fascinates people!"

Charlie then told his audience that he had discovered a special vegetation, direct from the West Indies. "All yer 'ave to do is rub the vegetation on yer corns or yer bunions, first thing in the morning and last thing at night." Charlie spent the whole day rubbing his bare foot with bits of banana. "And do yer know," he says, "I do believe it did me plates a bit o' good, strewth I do!"

Charlie made enough money that day to down his usual half dozen and buy himself a hot meal too! People could be so gullible!

There were plenty of others in the market who traded on that fact. If there was money to be made by playing a simple trick on people's credulity, then there was no shortage of tryers.

The Envelope Man springs immediately to mind — he had nothing but a suitcase full of small envelopes. He held them up, and in front of a fast-gathering crowd, he would put an Ingersoll watch in one, two half-crowns in another, and in the third, a ten shilling note. Then he would challenge anyone to buy any two of these envelopes for one shilling (5p). There was a skirmish as several people fought to buy them but nobody ever got the "treasure" — they usually ended up with a tuppenny trinket instead!

Perhaps the most flamboyant and well known trickster was Prince Monolulu, the racing tipster. He strode around the market, usually followed by a crowd of kids who were fascinated by his colourful appearance. He carried small, folded up pieces of paper on which was supposed to be the name of a horse that was a "dead cert". There must be many folk who still remember his famous cry:

I gotta horse, I gotta horse!
An old she horse
Plenty on there and plenty on there!
God makes the bees
The bees make the honey
The bookies take the money
I gotta horse!

Who could resist a tanner in the hope of procuring a windfall? More often than not though, the bits of paper were blanks!

It is said that 'Prince Monolulu' was no more than a stowaway on a boat from Ethiopia. Once he had made it to England, he found his own way of making a living. He worked at all the London markets and was often seen around at Hyde Park Corner too. Nobody seemed to mind even if he wasn't a real prince. Did it matter? Not really, for if nothing else, he played the part to perfection.

Those who sold their wares in the market were as diverse as those who came to stroll, look and buy. Some stall-holders were there to carry on the tradition of their parents and their grandparents before them. Others came because they thought they were in with a chance of making money, while others were simply down on their luck and came as a last resort.

"Miss Leon" was a pseudonym for a Polish lady of title. She was a countess but that was something she preferred to keep

44

to herself. When she first came to The Cally, she couldn't even afford her own pitch — she shared with others until she felt confident to go it alone at 2/3d (11p) a time.

"I like Japanese prints and Chinese things. In my country, I was educated in Oriental art so I have a feeling for exotic things," she said. One day, she acquired a set of Chinese bowls with floral china spoons. She set them out lovingly on her stall, secretly hoping not to sell them, but along came an American tourist and spied them almost immediately.

"How much are those bowls?" asked the tourist.

"One guinea," (£1.05) answered Miss Leon, hoping that the price might be too much.

"Gee! That's a lot of money," said the American lady, stroking one of the bowls carefully. "What's the lowest price you'll take for them?"

"I'll take twenty one shillings," (£1.05) offered Miss Leon.

"Done!" cried the tourist, counting out her twenty one shillings, while the spoons and bowls were wrapped up in newspaper for her.

"But I wasn't always that smart," says Miss Leon, recollecting her early days when the dealers were constantly on the alert for a bargain and to fool anyone who wasn't quite so quick witted.

"I once paid thirty shillings (£1.50) for a carved brown jade fish and then tried to resell it for more, but somebody chanced by and told me that it was soapstone and not jade and that I had been tricked. A second person told me the very same thing, so feeling dispirited, I sold it to him for thirty shillings — the price I had just paid, so I didn't lose anything."

The very next week, her 'customer' returned and said, "By the way, that fish of yours that I bought last week turned out to be real jade! I made myself a tenner!" Poor Miss Leon — she learnt her trade the hard way.

Baronet Sir John Stuart Knell, son and grandson of two London Lord Mayors, was 51 years old when things went badly wrong and he lost all his money. He took to sweeping the streets of Chelsea on a Sunday for 5/8d (28p) and to make a few extra bob, he ran a stall at The Cally. Nobody knew him by name, or his real identity — all his mates there called him 'Dad'.

To end up with a pitch on The Stones after living on a 2000 acre estate in Hertfordshire where he had kept servants, chauffeur driven cars and a wardrobe of fifty suits on an income of £4,000 per year, must have been tough, but Sir John was a resilient character. On a good day, he could pick up an extra pound or two.

"Sometimes, I've been without a single meal for two days," he said, "and the only suit I have now is the one on my back, but I'm happier now than I've ever been. I've found the love of a good woman!"

This tall handsome man had blue eyes that twinkled when he talked about his 'good woman'. Mending old china and painting it himself kept him happily occupied.

"Money can't buy everything," he said. "I'm penniless now, but I've got more friends here than I ever had when I was rich. But this is a strange place for a third Baronet to end up in!"

A strange place indeed to find a third Baronet, a Polish Countess and an Ethiopian Prince, but that was the way of life at The Cally.

Chapter Six

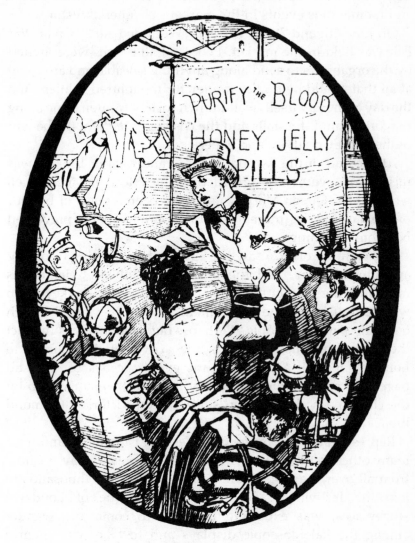

"An air of bonhomie and jollity hovered over all . . . . they were heady days in the summer of '26"

Perhaps the grand Royal opening day in 1855 was the only time that The Cally was to see such pageantry, pomp and splendour, but there were other exciting days and momentous events in the market's chequered history.

On June 6th and 7th in 1916, the Wounded Allies Great War Fair was held in the market. People of all classes were invited by the organisers to send along anything saleable and anything at all that would help raise money for the injured soldiers. On the day of the Fair itself, well-known society women came along to work behind the stalls and the costers gave them the benefit of their shrewd advice and experience.

At the end of the two days, the grand total of £30,000 was raised and everybody agreed that the effort had been well worthwhile. Queen Mary would have been a guest of honour on the day, but the untimely death of Lord Kitchener prevented her from attending . . .

The summer of 1926 saw the Silver Jubilee of King George V and Queen Mary, and the prospect of Jubilee Celebrations infiltrated the market so that the stall-holders were keyed up with enthusiasm and excitement. Were they really such fervently patriotic people? Perhaps. But more likely is the fact they were anxiously awaiting the arrival of the tourists to London for such a great historic event. Scenes of splendid pageantry and ceremony and gay festivities were about to hit the city on a scale not seen since Queen Victoria's Diamond Jubilee.

Representatives from the Colonies and Dominions and from many other countries were arriving in town every day. Visitors from all over the globe were pouring in in their thousands to join the festivities, and The Cally, as one of London's showplaces, was expecting them all to come and wander among the kaleidoscopic displays and to take with them a souvenir of London — something special, something British. The opportunity was there for everyone to make some extra cash and extra sales. It was a time of optimism after several lean years during which market takings had dwindled and slumped. No wonder the stall-holders were excited!

Everybody was making that little extra effort. Tea services in Dresden and Worcester china graced the stalls. Floral vases, beautiful enamelled jewellery boxes and crystal-mounted lustres vied for a special place on display. Objets d'art glistened and twinkled in the sunlight. These were the sort of things that would attract the attention and the currency of the overseas visitors.

A week or so before Jubilee Day itself, the atmosphere changed tangibly. The visitors began to flock through the gates, beautifully attired in colourful gowns, hats and shoes. Handsome gentleman escorted their ladies in among the stalls and bought them jewellery, souvenirs and all manner of finery, while many a mamma needed her parasol to protect her lily white skin from the bright sunshine.

A profusion of different tongues could be heard, all vying for attention in excited confusion. Those that couldn't speak English made themselves and their requests understood by wild gesticulations.

What a change from the dreary, long and meagre winters and the wearying summers of recent years. The flower stalls were doing a prolific trade. All the ladies were carrying huge bunches of red roses and carnations of every hue. The ice-cream salesmen couldn't keep up with the demand for wafers and cornets. New tea stalls appeared on the Stones — bright green iron tables with clean white cloths and posies of flowers sprung up overnight . . . and did a roaring trade. It was strawberry time, and everybody, everywhere was partaking without exception.

Along with all the tourists, familiar faces could be spotted amongst the crowds — those of Dolores Costello, Edmund Lowe, Sylvia Sidney, Edward Everett Horton, Zazu Pitts, Greta

Garbo, Bebe Daniels and Ben Lyon, and other such celebrities of the stage and silver screen. Great was the excitement when they were recognised, followed and pursued by an excited crowd.

Day after day, the sun shone down on the Stones and an air of bonhomie and jollity hovered over all. The mood was infectious and everyone was happy.

They were heady days in the summer of '26.

Edward, Prince of Wales, made a notable visit to the market on the 23rd October 1929, a visit made without any pomp and ceremony. He was however, invited to inspect the cleanliness and sanitary conditions of the abattoirs in which he showed great interest, and he asked if he could mark a flank of home-killed beef with the National Mark. A ladder was duly bought along for him and the Prince climbed up to mark the beef — an action which resulted in loud applause. That side of beef was later sold in aid of St. Bartholomew's Hospital.

Occasionally, a VIP would turn up at The Cally unannounced, and in no time at all, the news had filtered all around the Stones. Sir Percy Greenaway, Lord Mayor of London, took himself on a surprise shopping spree in June 1933. First stopping at Mr. Elston's china stall, he had a long conversation on the subject of English bone china and Dresden figurines. Next, two gypsies ventured to persuade him to buy some oilcloth, but they hadn't got quite what he wanted. Finally, he bought a Japanese penknife and seemed well pleased with his purchase, but by this time, the crowds were thronging about him and it was no longer possible to shop in peace. Thus, he made his escape.

The Princess Royal, Princess Mary, did rather better on her visit in May 1934. She managed to stroll among the stalls for nearly an hour with her ladies in waiting before she was recognised. In a tan walking suit, and a small felt hat pulled down over her face, she made mostly for the antique jewellery stalls, browsing and fingering items that caught her attention. She purchased a small pomade pot bearing a portrait of her grandfather, the Prince Consort, on the lid. Mr. B. Shaw, after selling the pot to her, thought she looked vaguely familiar . . .

Mr. Gould had a fine silver filigree necklace on display which caught her fancy. Not wanting to try it on herself, she held it against the neck of her maid, but she seemed a little unsure. Perhaps she could call back and buy it later — if there was nothing she liked better?

The Princess tried several other stalls looking at trinkets, but by this time, the whisper was gaining momentum and the crowd pressing at her back was growing in size. Hurriedly, she slipped into the flower market section and out into Market Road again where her chauffeur driven car was waiting for her. She never did go back to buy Mr. Gould's silver filigree necklace . . .

Exciting events and Royal visits always caused enough of a stir in the community to warrant a mention in the national press, but there were other times when more infamous deeds made the headlines too. Stories of stampeding cows, besieged bulls and drunken drovers were often reported in the newspapers and will forever be remembered and handed down from generation to generation.

Perhaps the funniest of these is the story of the besieged bull that took fright and ran into Camden Dwellings before finally getting stuck on the roof! Let Mr. E.G. Hills tell the story, after all, he was an eye-witness at the time:

"It was August 1912. I was only about 10 or 12 years old at the time, and my mum had sent me to the butchers in St. Pauls Road. It was very early in the morning, and as I was walking along York Way, a large herd of cattle was being driven to the slaughterhouses. As they got to Market Road, they didn't seem to want to turn down it, and the drover was yelling, 'Turn 'em back! Turn 'em back!'

"I wasn't quite sure what to do, so I went 'Whoosh!' at them, but instead of turning them back, that scattered them in all directions. The drover was joined by a mate and together they frantically tried to round them up, but one stupid bull took it into his head to run into Camden Dwellings.

"A couple of old women were coming down the steps at the time and they came face to face with the brute so they screamed blue murder and ran for their lives back upstairs! The bull went after them and the drovers were chasing the bull. It wasn't half a commotion!

"Eventually it got itself stuck on the stairs, so a lot of pushing and hooting went on, and finally they got it up on the roof where it went berserk, charging at all the washing blowing in the breeze and bringing all the washing lines down!

"Now, I was supposed to be doing the errands and then going off to school, but I couldn't miss all that excitement, could I? So I bunked off school, and went back!

"When I got back, there was a huge crowd of police, drovers, housewives and kids, and a photographer, trying to get a picture of this bull, sitting with all the washing lines round it and a pair of grandma's knickers on its head! But every time the photographer tried to get near, the bull charged, so the photographer packed up and ran!

"At last, one policeman came along with a rifle. One shot, and that was that. The end of the poor old bull. Then the problem was how to get the thing down. They couldn't lift it down the stairs — it was too big! There was only one thing for it — throw it over the top! So that's the way it went. Half a dozen of them there drovers and policemen picked it up and slung it off the roof. It didn't half go down with a thud, and it broke a couple of paving stones too!"

Another humorous incident happened in August 1926, although it might not have been so funny for those involved at the time . . . for the headlines told the story as "Bull Fight in Islington!"

It appears that 35 West Highland steers arriving at Holloway Road LNER station en route to the market, ran amok and careered around the surrounding streets for more than an hour before they could be rounded up. The police took on the role of picadors while the drovers themselves were the matadors of the round up, and the traffic was held up as far as Kings Cross!

There were casualties too — three men and one boy were injured during the proceedings. Mrs. Popworth was pushing baby May in her pram around Kings Cross when she got the shock of her life. Baby May (if she was old enough to know any nursery rhymes at the time) might have grown up believing in them, for she was laying there, gurgling happily, when a cow jumped over her pram! Fortunately, she was not hurt, but poor Mrs. Popworth passed out on the spot!

Another stray animal charged at a policeman in York Way. The policeman side-stepped and caught it by the horns. Afterwards, he could not actually recall doing that. "It must have been instinct" he commented when interviewed by the press. He suffered a severely bruised hand for his efforts, but nevertheless, he became a local hero!

A third bull deposited itself appropriately in front of a hoarding advertising Bovril and defied anybody to come near it. Nobody did! At length, finding it all very boring, it began to charge at the passing horses and carts.

The thundering herd, with bloodshot eyes and foaming mouths, managed to cover two miles during the afternoon before the drovers from York Way managed to get them all under control. Finally, even the last one was rounded up and taken to Maiden Lane where they were all safely penned for the rest of the day, and everybody breathed a sigh of relief.

Market days were long over in 1952, but the Corporation of London abbatoirs in Market Road were still in use. There must be many, many people today who have vivid childhood memories of the cattle, groaning and lurching their way from the railway sidings in Piper Close to the slaughterhouses where they were driven to their fate.

Around seven hundred people may be able to recall a wintry afternoon in January 1952, when as children, they were trapped inside their primary school in Copenhagen Street while a mad cow cavorted in their playground outside. Anxious mums waited outside the gates watching the spectacle while a hundred little giggling faces peered out, noses pressed against the classroom windows! Mr. Roser, the school caretaker, was the first to see the cow racing down Boadicea Street, followed by a van and six drovers in hot pursuit.

Mr. Roser turned and fled into the school grounds, forgetting to shut the gate behind him. The cow gave chase and charged through the 'Boys' entrance. Poor Mr. Roser leapt up the steps two at a time with the cow at his heels, but fortunately, he managed to slam the school door shut behind him! As he leant against it, his heart beating violently, he couldn't help but chuckle at his wild west type, narrow escape!

For two hours, the cow pranced around the playground, thoroughly enjoying itself and its evasion of capture. Ropes strung across the playground failed to trap him. The six drovers hovered at the school's edges with lassoos at the ready, but every time they homed in on the animal, it charged and sent them scattering. Finally, Charlie Collins, hero of the day, climbed up on to the school roof and managed to drop a noose over its neck, and the cow's frolics were over.

The animal was escorted back to the slaughterhouse and the children came out of school with a thoroughly exciting tale to take home to their mums!

There are so many amusing and colourful stories told, but only the strangest and the funniest found their way into the newspapers. For those that were recorded, there are at least a hundred more — not quite lost forever just yet, for they live in the minds of the people who were there at the time — the stall-holders, the shoppers and the families who lived on the spot.

Theirs were the children who roamed the market, shrewd enough to earn themselves a penny here and a penny there, fetching cups of tea and pushing loaded barrows; theirs were the kids who scraped their knees whilst climbing to peer over the walls of the animal lairs, and who used dried out pigs' bladders to kick around the streets, for want of a decent football!

Those same children who played on the streets from dawn till dusk in the shadow of the market railings, breathing in the rarefied bovine air which blended nicely with the aromas from Henson's tripe factory, are today's senior citizens. They are the ones who live to tell the tales today. Their bodies may be frailer today in keeping with their age, but their minds are still as sharp as the proverbial two-edged sword, and their memories of market life are as clear today as they were yesterday.

In fact, ask them about life Up The Cally, and it seems like it was only yesterday . . .

MY MOTHER, & AUNTS, TOLD
US OF THE ANIMAL ON THE ROOF!
— BACK IN 1930's! — IT BECAME
A FAMILY TALE!
THEY OFTEN SPOKE OF THE
HERDS DRIVEN UP LEIGHTON RD.,
IN 1900/10. INCL. GEESE!

Chapter Seven

"The kids used all the canniness and wit they possessed to evade the weekly jaunts of the truant officer!

Those streets which backed onto the square mile of the market — Corinth Road, Goodinge Road, Surr Street, Halse Street and Fakenham Terrace, were lined with tiny two-up, two-down houses which boasted outside loos. In those houses lived the families typical of the area and of the latter years of Victorian England, each with at least half a dozen children and barely two ha'pennies to rub together: families such as the Corkes and the Bowmans.

The lads of these families were born into the familiarity of Friday market on their doorstep, and to them, Fridays represented the chance to earn a few pennies, the chance to scavenge among the stalls for any leftovers, but even more exciting was the chance to skip a day's schooling and to use all the canniness and wit they possessed to evade the weekly jaunts of the truant officer!

Charlie Bowman was one of those lads who earned his pocket money in the market. He can recall those far-off days with a cheerful smile. Today, he lives on a smart housing estate in Banbury, Oxfordshire, but he was born at number 5, Corinth Road and spent all of his early years in the market area.

"How well I can remember the crush at the market gates as the clock struck ten. I used to earn myself a few coppers by climbing over the railings to run and get a pitch for someone. In the fruit market we'd collect empty wooden boxes that were left behind and sell them for firewood. I remember too, collecting up all the old newspapers and cardboard after the market on Fridays, and then pushing it all in a big bundle, up to the waste paper merchants at the top of North Road on Saturday mornings. That money provided me with pocket money for Saturday morning pictures and sweets!

"I once had a cousin who ran an old junk stall. I used to help him sell it all — anything on the ground for a penny! He had lots of old pictures and I used to lay them out on the pitch of someone who had packed up and gone home. One day, an old gentleman came along and asked the price of a certain picture. I said 'how much will you give me for it?' He studied it closely and said 'I'll give you a pound.' I replied 'Give me two pound and you can have the lot!' I got my two pound, but he only took the one picture. Goodness knows what it was really worth!

"There was a man in the market with a cowboy hat — a real ten gallon stetson, and he sold sweets. My pal and I would crawl up on our hands and knees through the legs of people crowding around the stall and come out with a pocket full of sweets from underneath! I used to do the washing up at tea stalls too, to earn a few more pennies, or I'd help load up the carts and lorries when it was time to go home. The loading up was a laugh — we'd put some stuff on the carts and some underneath it. Then we'd wait until they drove off, and anything left behind was ours!"

With all the attractions and excitement of a big market like The Cally and all the opportunities it afforded young lads like Charlie to earn some pocket money, it was no wonder that there was a noticeable lack of boys in school on a Friday! Charlie went to the Brecknock School and then to Hungerford, but he can remember many a Friday when he 'wasn't well'.

"One day, when my pal and I were looking at some stuff on a stall, someone tapped me on the shoulder. 'What? No school today boys?' We answered 'no', whereupon the gent asked 'What school do you go to?' We told him, the Brecknock. 'Well I'm the school inspector,' said the gent, and with that, you couldn't see our backsides for dust!

"I have a laugh today when I think about all the pranks we did get up to, but being not very well off, it gave me the chance to earn a little spending money, and that was something not many parents could afford to give to their kids in those days."

Robert Beasley from Beckenham in Kent, has vivid memories of his boarding school days at St. Aloysius College in Highgate. With his friend, Norman Lee Wilson, Robert broke bounds from school one day and wandered off in the direction of Holloway and The Cally.

They had a marvellous time, rummaging through the various bric a brac stalls and listening to the patter of the salesmen, but the biggest find of the day was an old bicycle — on sale for 10/6d (52p). Norman and Robert counted out every penny they possessed between them, and they found they had enough. The bike was theirs, so joyfully, they took it in turns to ride it back to Highgate. Unfortunately, a teacher was lying in wait for them after their day's escapade and they were suitably chastised for their act of truancy!

The following week, the two lads were off to Hove with a group from school for a seaside holiday. Naturally, the bicycle went too, and it gave the boys a great deal of pleasure during their holiday.

Eventually though, the novelty of the old bike wore off. Robert and Norman returned to school and decided to sell their bike to a day boy — for the grand sum of 12/6d (62p). "All told," says Robert, "a thoroughly satisfactory transaction indeed!"

Tommy Bush, another senior citizen, lives near Essex Road today, not too far from his early origins in the streets around the Cattle Market. As a lad, Tommy loved animals and he can remember being sent by his mum to fetch a jug of fresh milk from the animal lairs. Many were the times when that simple errand extended into an hour's fun, for Tommy used to sneak behind the fountain and past the lairmen to climb onto the cattle sheds and look through at the cows. The animals were waiting patiently, tied with ropes to the rings at the back of the lairs. (The odd one or two of those brass rings and the places they occupied can still be seen today on the walls at the back of the Astroturf).

Tommy cannot remember now just how many times he was scolded for returning home late with torn clothes, grazed knees and a chipped milk jug! But the scoldings did not deter him from getting up to more mischief . . .

On Saturday nights, the meat was taken from the market down to Smithfield in lorries covered with tarpaulins. Tommy can remember hiding behind the lorries with several other lads, and just as the engines started, the lads would all jump on the back of the lorries and sneak a ride! The idea was to see who could hang on the longest — before the bumps in North Road shook them off! Tommy once made it right to the corner of Caledonian Road — and jumped off as the lorry turned the corner. Luckily, he was never hurt, but there are plenty of 'old boys' around who can recall the bruises, sprains and broken arms received in that way!

Henry Corke is another great old veteran of The Cally, living in 'Henry's Castle' at Finsbury Park. Henry's name was well known around The Cally. He lived in Halse Street as a child, and in his later years, he had an antique shop in Caledonian Road.

One of Henry's earliest recollections is of the day when the besieged bull was thrown from the roof of Camden Dwellings; another concerns his own front door — he can vividly remember the gaping hole left in the wood made by an angry bull charging along Halse Street! His dad could not afford a new door, nor could he mend the hole, so for a long time, the wind whistled through the hole and a piece of string held the door in place!

61

Henry remembers earning his pocket money in the same way as the other lads, but what fascinated him most were the carved animal heads at the top of each pillar, all around the market. When the market had closed down at the beginning of the war, the local residents woke up one morning to find that all these animal heads had disappeared overnight. The story goes that they turned up in an antique shop in Blackstock Road, Finsbury Park, and from there, they were shipped off to America where they were mounted on wooden blocks, painted gold and sold as souvenirs.

Somehow or other, nine of these heads found their way into Henry's antique shop, and they were his pride and joy. He polished them regularly and kept them in a safe place, until one day, he asked a friend to mind the shop while he went out. On his return, Henry found his friend rubbing his hands with glee. "I've made you a fortune," he said. "I've sold all those animal heads to one customer!" Needless to say, Henry's comments are not fit to be recorded here for posterity!

Harry Davis, now retired to a country cottage in Rye, can cast his mind back over 66 years to a vivid recollection of being dumped unceremoniously on top of a barrow full of goods, and being pushed by his older brother from Wharfedale Road in Kings Cross to the market. Once there, his mother set up her stall on a pitch and sat young Harry down on the cobbles with a tray of thimbles to sell at a penny each. This kept him occupied for a little while, but sooner or later, Harry would toddle away through the crowds and find his way to the slaughterhouses to watch a bit of the action. Then, his presence being discovered, one of the slaughtermen would return him to his mother in the market!

Many of the two wheel barrows that were loaded up and trundled to market doubled up as stalls from which goods were sold. Those who could afford an extra bob or two, rented barrows like these from a proprietor in Marquis Road. Quite often, stallholders who had rented the barrows and sold all their goods, could not be bothered to return them, so for a mere ha'penny, kids like Frank Guiver, would drag them from the market, push them into Market Road, and back up the hill to the owner.

Half a dozen lads would fight over each barrow — it was a cut throat operation to see who could return the most barrows at a spanking pace. Heaven help the weakest kids! Having earnt as many ha'pennies as possible from trundling barrows, Frank and his mates would return to the market to scavenge among the empty stalls for fallen sweets, damaged fruit, and shrimps that had been dropped from the fish stalls. With arms full of goodies and wooden boxes to sit on, these lads would return to a secret hideout behind Queens Mansions and have a "scrumper's feast"! Says Frank, "Why we never suffered from serious food poisoning after these incidents, God only knows!"

Albert Paxton of Thane Villas, loves reminiscing about those far-off market days: "When I was a boy, about eight years old, I used to wake up early at about 5.30 a.m. and go to see the cows arrive. I lived in Roman Road then (now Roman Way), behind the police station. I used to take a stick with me and go to meet the first arrival of cows at the sidings. As the drovers herded them up North Road, I used to run along behind and give the cows a tap with my stick to get them moving along!

"Then on a Friday, I'd play truant from school and earn myself a few pennies. I'd run along to the bottom of Market Road and help one of the costers push their barrow up the hill. I got tuppence for that, then I'd go back and help another one for another tuppence. At ten o'clock, one of the costers would give me his jacket and his two shillings (10p) fee for the pitch and I'd rush in through those gates and grab his pitch for him until he got there with his barrow!

"During the day, I'd go round the stalls and fetch jugs of tea for a penny. It was always packed and very noisy up there, but I loved it. I went every Friday. I hated school. I'd much rather be up at the market earning a few pennies. In the evening, when the market was closing down, I'd still be there, helping to pack up. I used to help stack up the tables and load them on to a barrow, then sit on top and hold them tight as they were pushed along. Then I'd go back to the market to see what else I could do, but by then, I'd be so tired, and I often sat down against the railings and fell asleep! If I hadn't arrived home by the time it was getting dark, my dad used to come up the market looking for me!

"Another thing I remember so well is the police coming along to round up all the drunks. There was always plenty of them! The police picked them up, dumped them in the wagon, and carted them off to the police station. At the corner of Roman Way, opposite the police station, there used to be a coffee shop called Snooks, and old Mr. Snook had the contract for providing the meals for the drunks. I often used to see him carrying all the food across the road to the police station.

"Looking back on those times now, it seems like another world. When I think of the kids today, and the expensive toys they get, and the amusements they have, I do tend to feel sorry for them . . . they've missed out on an awful lot of fun. Some of the best days of my life were spent at The Cally."

George Hughes hails from Upminster in Essex and when recalling his days at The Cally, remembers his fascination with the "con men". How well he remembers the Envelope Man with the ten shilling note, half crown and watch. One Friday morning, having earned himself a few bob during the week, he plucked up enough courage to buy two envelopes for a shilling (5p) — but he didn't strike lucky. Like so many others before him, George found a cheap trinket inside each one!

There was another fellow who often caught young George's attention — another con man who always managed to gather a crowd around him. "In this envelope," said the con man, "is a wonderful book with some amazing pictures. This is a book for adults. Not children, not juveniles, but only adults. I must be careful who I sell this book to because it's only for broadminded, worldly people. I can't sell it to prudes or to anybody who might be shocked. That's why I only sell this book in a sealed envelope and I urge you not to open it or even break the seal of the envelope until you are far away from here and on your own. That way, you won't shock anybody else, and you can enjoy the book in private!"

Poor George was often sorely tempted to buy the envelope and peer at the 'naughty' pictures inside. But as he recalls, somebody he knew bought an envelope one day and George got a long-awaited glimpse . . . inside the envelope were a few printed pages from the Bible and a coloured text of scripture!

These sort of con men used to regale the crowds with their tales, sell as many of their wares as they could, then pack up and disappear to another corner of the market before anybody could complain and before any 'coppers' could catch up with them. Just occasionally though, a policeman would question or caution a dishonest trader, and within seconds, the news would spread like wildfire and a crowd would appear as if from nowhere! At the front of that crowd would be half a dozen kids, arms waving, voices shouting, cheering or jeering either party on.

How those back street kids loved a spectacle like that!

Chapter Eight

"Many a tale abounds of priceless treasures that were found amongst the junk stalls and the rubbish laid out on the stones"

Many a tale abounds of priceless treasures that were found in the Caledonian Market amongst the junk stalls and the rubbish laid out on the stones. Some finds were of such significant interest and value that they were worth reporting in the national press.

On January 19th, 1932, the Morning Post reported that one such bargain hunter experienced the luckiest day of her life . . .

The lady in question was searching for a particular string of dark beads to match a recently purchased cocktail dress. She had searched high and low, through every shop in the West End, but nothing had taken her fancy at all. One of her long-suffering friends, growing tired of the fruitless shopping expeditions, offered to take her along to the Caledonian Market. "If you can't find anything there," said her friend, "you might as well give up."

Together, they searched the jewellery stalls around the market, and finally, the lady came upon a row of beads. They were exactly what she wanted, but she was most indignant when the vendor asked for seven and sixpence (37p)! Although she badly wanted the beads, there was no way she was going to pay such an exorbitant price!

However, throughout the week, our lady could not get those beads out of her mind and finally, the following Friday, she returned to the market and sought out the same jewellery stall. Fortunately, the necklet was still for sale. She duly paid her seven and sixpence and took her beads away, happy at last.

The following evening, our heroine donned her new cocktail dress, powdered her nose and arranged the dark beads around her pretty neck and set off to a banquet. As luck would have it, her table companion was one of the most distinguished jewellers in London.

For a time, they conversed politely, the jeweller's eyes roaming frequently to the sparkling necklace until at length, he could contain his curiosity no longer. He requested a closer look at the beads on the pretext of examining the loose safety clasp. The beads glistened in his shaking hands as he turned them over and over again. He began to question the lady about their origin and price, and he could hardly believe his ears when she told him where she had bought them from.

That modest string of 'dark beads' picked up on a market stall for 7/6d were actually genuine black pearls and the very next day, they were sold for the princely sum of £20,000!

*   *   *

Some years ago, a somewhat absent-minded but skilled gem-stone craftsman designed and constructed a beautiful globe of the world with all the countries picked out entirely in opals. The intricacy of the work had taken hours of patient toil and the completed masterpiece was his pride and joy. He wrapped it carefully in layers of tissue paper and set out with it to London to try his luck at selling it.

At the station, he stopped at a tea shop for some sustenance before his journey. Sipping his tea, he was lost in dreams of the fame and fortune that his creation might bring him, when suddenly he realised that his train was at the platform. He jumped up, left his tea, and raced to the train, leaping into a carriage just as the guard blew the whistle. Leaning back breathlessly in his seat, he looked round for his precious parcel — and there it was, perched in the centre of the table in the tea shop . . .

Two years later, a young housewife in London chanced to hear the story of the missing hand-crafted opal globe as it was reported in the news. "Strange," she thought. "I have a similar beautiful ornament," and spurred on by the thought of the reward offered, she wrapped her 'ornament' carefully in a cloth and took it to Scotland Yard. The policeman eyed her suspiciously when she unwrapped her parcel before him. "Well young lady," he began. He inspected the globe thoroughly and recognised it immediately as the 'lost' article. "And where might you have found such a precious ornament, might I ask?"

"I bought it a couple of months ago," she answered in all honesty. "I picked it up at The Cally for fifteen bob!"

*   *   *

Townley Searle was a bookseller of good repute. In his modest shop, he had ancient and modern books from all corners of the earth, but his chief delight was searching for more books — ancient, interesting, unusual or otherwise. No matter what it was, Mr. Searle was always eager to add to his collection. Little wonder then, that he could often be seen haunting the bookstalls of markets such as The Cally.

One Friday morning, his persistence paid off. With his friend, a painter by name of John Flanagan, he roamed the market stalls for several hours. Imagine his delight when he came upon a rare copy of the first musical version of Alice in Wonderland. The book had been published at 6d a copy and it had been such a flop that only a very few copies were printed. Searle snapped it up for one penny and later, he sold it at a handsome profit — for £10.00!

*   *   *

Such stories, when reported in the press, only served to increase the popularity of The Cally. Ordinary folk reading them, got it into their heads that The Cally was a treasure trove — a place where there were rich pickings if only one took the time and trouble to look, and it added to the excitement and romanticism of a trip to the market on a Friday.

In actual fact, the 'finds' were fairly few and far between, but nevertheless, the stories pulled in the crowds and the crowds arrived full of enthusiasm, encouraging the stallholders to pile their pitches ever higher with goods and chattels for sale. There was no harm in setting off to The Cally with great expectations and high hopes. A day's rummaging amongst the bric a brac was good fun anyway, and who knew for sure what might just be found hidden innocently behind an old tin kettle or under a copper frying pan?

Many folk today remember the excitement with which they set off on a Friday and there are a lot of 'souvenirs' still around which can lay claim to being bought at The Cally.

John Bailey, originally from Archway but retired to Southgate now, has a few souvenirs in his possession, and vivid memories of rummaging through the market stalls:

"We loved foraging through all the stalls. There was such a wonderful variety of everything you could think of. My family have always been involved in amateur operatics, and they still are. We have managed to find the most odd items at the market — beautiful fans, for instance, for The Mikado. I still have a black whale-bone fan which I used in the role of Pish-Tush at school when I was 12. Another time, my mother bought enough wool offcuts of varying colours to re-knit into a Fair Isle pullover which I wore with the greatest pride to school for several years.

"On every visit, we never came home empty-handed. If it was too big for tram transport (Yes — a Number 17 tram!), then we walked."

From Ealing in West London, Ruby Witty can recall buying one of the most memorable items in her life from The Cally — her wedding dress:

"My mother always believed in buying good quality second hand articles rather than cheap shoddy new goods and she insisted on taking me to The Cally to buy my wedding dress when I was 18 years of age, although I would much rather have had a new one! My mother was a formidable lady, and we young people did as we were told in those days — without question.

"We found a wedding dress which satisfied her and after some discussion with the stall owner, she bought it for thirty shillings. This, of course, was more than we could have bought a new one for, but it was the quality that counted with Mother. It was exceedingly beautiful and I suppose it must have belonged to what we used to call 'One of the Quality'.

"It had two under petticoats of silk and net, one petticoat of taffeta which rustled, and the dress itself was of very soft pure silk trimmed with seed pearls around the neck, waist and sleeves. The embroidery was worked beautifully and of course, all done by hand.

"However, the problem for me was that it was full length and since this was just after the First World War, hemlines had crept up. The fashion was for a much shorter

length. After much discussion with my mother, she allowed me to take it up with three large tucks. Looking back at the old photos now, I can see Mother was right — it would have looked much more elegant worn full length — especially with my new husband in top hat and tails!

"The end of the dress, as far as I was concerned, was when I moved to Ealing to be near my youngest daughter. I gave the dress to her to sell in her little antique shop in Haven Lane. My daughter received £50.00 for it and the lady who bought it was absolutely delighted, saying that the trimmings alone were well worth the money.

"In fact, many are the bits and pieces which have found their way into her shop which originated from the old Caledonian Market. They still have a span of life in them — such was the quality of goods sold there."

Doreen Bazell hails from Woolwich these days, but as a young teenager, she went to The Cally with her mum very often on a Friday. "My mum once bought me a real posh coat there — a blue 'swagger'. It cost a pound, and came complete with a white flower in the button hole."

Doreen's coat lasted for a good few winters and then her mother put it at the back of the wardrobe. "Years later, when I was pregnant and had nothing to wear, mum gave me the blue coat again and I wore it throughout my pregnancy. How's that for a pound!

"Thinking back to The Cally is like looking back on another world. People try to tell us they were the bad old days. Don't you believe it — they were great days!"

Murielle Connolly remembers the same 'good old days' with a hint of nostalgia: "Those were the days when you did not have to lock your kitchen door every time you went into the garden! You could leave a bike outside your front door, and it would still be there in the morning!

"I remember the market so well. I did some of my shopping there in the 'twenties. I still have a copper pan that I bought there all those years ago. I remember a stall run by a man who used to bring a whole sack full of silk stockings. I suppose they must have been 'seconds', but they were 1/3d (8p) a pair. He used to empty the sack out in a heap on the stones and everybody would dive in and try to find a matching pair. On one occasion, a woman started on them before he was ready. He was furious! He picked up a small iron bar and shouted "'Ere! 'Ands off Clara Cook!" That sticks in my mind to this day!"

Irene Hogendoorn, from Harrow Weald today, remembers a time when she was taken on a number 14 bus from The Favourite in Hornsey Rise, to the market on a Friday. "I remember a man who sold gramophone records at one stall. He was quite talented and used to give a performance with each record he played. Sometimes he did impersonations or even a dance. We always spent a long time in front of his stall because there was plenty of laughter. Occasionally, he used theatre props too which made people laugh even more.

"I remember the large fresh-faced lady on the tea-stall beneath the Clock Tower, She made the 'best cup of tea in London'. Even as a child, I remember that that was almost true, because she put extra sugar and milk in for me!

"In the summer, I was treated to 'Hokey Pokey' — pink and white ice cream sold in blocks on a piece of paper and in the winter, I often had hot sarsaparilla.

"My mother liked wandering around the stalls, looking at the second hand stage clothes. There were crinoline dresses, ballet dresses, top hats and gent's evening wear with shoes to match. I often wondered who bought those sort of things.

"I think the thing that stands out most in my memory was the humour and the good natured fun. People in those days had very little, but they certainly knew how to live together and enjoy life, regardless of age, sex or creed. The Caledonian Market was home to one great big, happy family."

Doris Lloyd was only nine years old when she was taken to the market. Being a child, the sweet stalls were the biggest attraction for her: "My favourite stall was the one where the lady pulled toffee. It was a sight to behold and I must have stood for hours watching her pull it into a skein by using a metal rod. Then she would twist it and throw it up in the air, catch it and twist it again, then cut it into small pieces with a huge pair of scissors. She weighed these into triangular paper bags. I had some every week. Toffee has never tasted so good ever since!

"Living in Holloway, we visited the market every week, and usually stayed all day. I loved it when dusk began to fall and the stallholders lit their naptha flare lights. They made a lovely hissing noise and spurted out just like bright yellow blow torches. The whole place took on a magic atmosphere when it got dark."

Strange, how many folk can recall the variety of food that was on sale at The Cally . . . Irene's Hokey Pokey, Doris, with her memories of toffee . . . Vera Comber from Hornchurch in Essex writes: "I think there used to be an old tram in the market that served as a refreshment stall. People could sit inside or on the top deck and have a breather while eating. We always had to wait until the end of the day, when all the shopping was done before we were allowed to go to our own special tea stall — the one which sold huge cheese cakes with plenty of shredded coconut on top. Scrumptious!

"My mother bought six second hand wooden dining chairs for 15/- (75p). We had to carry them back down North Road and try to get them home on the tram! My mum used to polish them each week and they looked great. When my sister and I got married, Mum gave us three of those chairs each to start our own homes. I then gave my three chairs to my own daughter, and she was still using them up until 1975 when she had to sell them before emigrating to Canada. They were still in perfect condition even then."

Still a Londoner today, Patrick O'Leary remembers his childhood days in York Way. His father and uncle ran a haulage business, A. and E. O'Leary, and rented a yard which backed on to the market. In the 1920's, the business was running lorries, horses and vans, and it was fascinating to a young boy to see the farrier at work in his forge. A goat called Billy guarded the premises at night and Billy was notorious for his fierceness — and for his yearning for the Great Beyond. Many times he escaped from the premises — much to the annoyance of the local police.

"I can remember Father William Attree, the parish priest of Copenhagen Street. He used to scour the market for any chalices and other bits of church plate which had somehow 'lost their way' on to the market stalls. His greatest concern was to buy them all, thus rescuing them from being put to secular use."

Living in Harrow today, Albert Pratley can recall "the best suit I ever bought" as coming from The Cally.

"I frequently visited that old market in the 'twenties. I earned about one pound a week, so I had to look for somewhere cheap to buy clothes. I once saw a stallholder serve a man with a jacket which was obviously far too big for him. The customer put it on and the stallholder simply grabbed hold of a handful of material in the middle of the back! The customer went off with his purchase, seemingly well satisfied!

"Of course, you had to see some of the slick performers at work. They seemed to be mostly of Jewish extraction and needed to be watched very closely indeed. One time, a friend of mine went to The Cally to buy a pair of trousers. When he arrived home, he unwrapped his parcel to find a pair of lady's bloomers instead!

"Sometimes we would bait the stallholders by asking them for an article, and after haggling with them for a long time, we would walk away, saying we did not want it after all! Then they would get really mad after trying so hard to flog something! But then, when you are eighteen or so, devilment is always on the cards.

"The brown suit I bought in The Cally for two pounds was easily the best one I ever bought. Luckily, I took a colleague with me to buy it, and to see that the stallholder did not grab a handful of jacket and say 'That eez a luverly fit'!"

Annie and Joseph Secchi live in Penn Road, Holloway today with their daughter Maria and her family, but in 'the good old days', they lived at number 20, North Road. Joseph recalls going over to the market on Fridays, taking the children with him. Maria was only four years old but she can remember the hubbub and the excitement of the market crowds. One day, Joseph found a brass razor which he bought for 3d from Charlie Barham, a great old market character who used to push a bassinet pram full of old junk up to his pitch every Friday.

Joseph still has his brass razor today but needless to say, he doesn't use it for shaving these days — it sits on the mantel shelf along with the rest of his wife's brass collection. Annie proudly shows off a heavy brass ring given to her by one of the drovers, and demonstrates how neatly it clips open for threading through the bull's nose. A little piece of living history which gleams brightly in pride of place in the firelight.

Only little things, yet ones which folk have cherished over the years, along with their memories and the tales of market life. Tales of the bargains they found for themselves, and tales of goods that lasted for many a long year. These objects of sentimental value such as John Bailey's fan, Albert Bowman's ancient typewriter that still works today, and Annie's bull ring, might not be worth much, but these folk wouldn't part with them for the world.

It was the mere hope of finding an exciting bargain or a valuable antique that sent people flocking to The Cally in their thousands. Perhaps Olga Prendergast has the right word for it. She remembers one of her mother's eccentric Hampstead friends saying, "My Dear! Let's go to the Hunting Ground!"

Chapter Nine

*"What wonderful, warm-hearted stories there are, all recalled
by folk who were there at the time . . ."*

The 'Hunting Ground' provided a rich and varied source of entertainment and excitement for Londoners during the years between the two Great Wars — thanks to the stallholders who always managed to unearth an amazing variety of different goods for sale each week.

There were upwards of two thousand market stalls at The Cally in its heyday, and although we have already encountered the eccentricities of some of the more colourful traders in the market, there were many more "ordinary" folk who were there to eke out a living, or to earn an extra honest bob or two. For those who were still trading on the eve of war in 1939, time has marched steadily on, yet there are still some folk scattered around who can reminisce of those times, fifty years ago, when they ran a stall at The Cally, or perhaps helped their parents in the busier times.

Evelyn Smithers, a grand old lady of 87 from Twickenham, recalls her childhood days when she went to the market to help on her grandparents' stall: "My grandparents used to have a large stall in Caledonian Market. They owned a china and glass shop in Kentish Town Road and every Tuesday and Friday we went to market with the trolley drawn by two lovely white horses called Tommy and Snowball. The trolley was laden with china and glass — ornaments, chamber pots, water jugs and such like. I was allowed to hold the reins of the horses on the way there, and grandma's large bulldog used to sit up on the trolley next to me! Once everything was all set up on display in the market, it was my job to go and fetch the jugs of tea."

The china trade was a popular one — Philip Reason remembers his stall there very well, although he came to be a market trader almost by accident. In 1928, he bought an old antique business, purely for the lease on the building. When clearing the shop out, he found the previous owners had left behind a pile of rubbish and the dustmen refused to take it away. Philip decided to take it all down to the market to try and get rid of it. He duly set up his stall, and within minutes, antique dealers were flocking all around him, picking over all the goods. He was astonished at the prices he was being offered for his 'rubbish' and it wasn't too long before his stall was empty and he was sixty pounds better off!

Not only is Mr. Reading still in Islington today, but he can remember his stall number — Q 26! Mr. Reading stocked toys, tools and any other cheap, end of line goods that he could get hold of from warehouses for re-sale. His most vivid recollection is of the day when he arrived at The Cally with a job lot of rubber ducks and big fish. No sooner had he blown them all up and set them out on the ground when a terrific thunderstorm started and the rain poured down in torrents. To keep himself dry, he sat underneath a big tarpaulin. When the rain had stopped, Mr. Reading emerged from his cover, only to find that all his rubber ducks and fish had swum away in the puddles and were happily floating off in the gulleys and down the drains!

"There was another chap beside me one day," says Mr. Reading, who had struggled up to the market with a large piano on a barrow. It must have weighed a ton, and he was worn out. He set the piano up and began to play some of the well-known tunes. People stood and watched, and sang along beside him, then moved on. For five hours, he played that piano on and off, hoping to sell it for fifty shillings (£2.50), but there were no takers. In the end he was so furious, so he set fire to the piano and walked away!"

Other folk had better luck with their wares though, and although they too had struggled to The Cally laden down with boxes, bags and crates, the homeward journey was often a whole lot easier. That's what usually happened for Sam Morris — well known in Islington today for his magnificent transformation of the Royal Agricultural Hall (known affectionately for years as The Aggie), into today's thriving Business Design Centre.

Sam was a schoolboy from London's East End in The Cally's heyday, but his dad took him out of school on Fridays because he needed an extra pair of hands to get the goods to market!

"My father Eddie was a job buyer, buying up old stock of anything. He would arrive home with boxes of redundant cosmetics, toiletries, remnants of cloth, clothing and artificial flowers. The artificial flowers came from milliner's stocks and they were especially good selling items — people needed a bit of colour in their homes in those days. The success of our weekly meals was often governed by dad's windfalls!

"Quite often, dad would need somebody to help him get to market and I was the only one who could go because my three elder brothers were out at work and the younger two were infants.

"Living near Bow underground station, the journey was a formidable one, and I, a five foot nothing twelve year-old, had to give dad a hand with the goods. This meant humping the heavy parcels by tying them together over my shoulders like a yoke. We started out at seven o'clock in the morning — a real 'crush hour' on the underground. We took the train to Whitechapel, changed to the Metropolitan line for Kings Cross, and then hopped on a tram up the Cally Road.

"I remember the trams so well — putting the parcels up the front by the driver, then nipping round the other side to get on before he drove away! Getting off, you had to be mighty quick to go round and collect the parcels again! Those tram rides with heavy parcels were enough to give anyone a nervous breakdown!

"We all crowded round the market gates waiting for them to open. My lack of height enabled me to worm my way through to the front and be one of the first in. Dad always favoured a pitch by the Clocktower, near the teas and the toilets. This corner was often regarded as the 'Oxford Street' of the market.

"We'd set everything up and literally use our best judgement to sell the stock, whether it was a pair of socks or a shirt. We'd take anything we could get. Sometimes Dad went off and left me in charge of the stall and I'd try and get him a good profit. We never completely sold out of everything, but the journey home was much easier.

"Being absent from school was tolerated by the masters — they usually understood the need for a youngster to help out in the family, so Morris being away from school on Fridays never caused a trauma. The masters gave a nod and a wink and wrote 'recurring bilious attacks' in the register!

"Although I missed a whole day's schooling every week, I'd say that I got another kind of education in that market. I learnt how to make a deal or two and keep my wits about me from an early age. I'd even go so far as to say that any market trader has it in him to become a good entrepreneur."

Wise words. As chairman and head of a major industrial company and the Business Design Centre, Sam has a few other schemes up his sleeve for more hotels and trade centres for the future. He's come a long way today from doing the odd deal in the shadow of the Clocktower and he has never forgotten the lessons he learned there.

George Driver came from Edgware originally and it was in Church Street market that he first came upon Chocolate Joe, and was offered a job — as Chocolate Joe's stooge: "I was only 17 years old at the time, and as I wandered through Church Street market in Edgware, I watched Chocolate Joe set up his stall. Suddenly, he called me over and said 'Hey young fellow, would you like a job working the markets with me?'

"I accepted gladly and my wages were fifteen shillings a week, plus a generous supply of sweets. We worked all the

London markets, but I particularly loved Fridays at The Cally. That one had the biggest crowds.

"I had to stand at the front of the stall, giving out the bags of sweets as Joe knocked them out at bargain prices. The idea was for Joe to make remarks about me which would make the customers laugh. He used to say 'What's the matter? You falling asleep down there George?' or 'Come on George, I've got a tortoise that moves faster than you!' or 'If you're that exhausted, I'll fetch a bed down next week, then you can get a bit of shuteye!'

"One day, we were all ready to start up when suddenly a vehicle backed into us. Our stall was knocked over and the sweets went flying in all directions! Next to us, the stamp stall was shattered too. There was the biggest free for all you ever saw — people fighting to get handfuls of stamps and sweets together! Poor old Joe — there were no profits for him that day!"

Mr. J. Munns from Tottenham beat George Driver to his first job by 7 years — he was only 10 when he landed a job at The Cally!

"I used to work on Fridays at The Cally for a man called Palmer of Club Row. He had a stall selling dogs, cats and chickens. It was my job to hold up a cute little puppy and say 'Lovely dogs and puppies from a shilling each'. When it was time to pack up, I got a ride on his horse and cart to Caledonian Road and then he'd pay me 3d (1½p) and two eggs. I spent my threepence like this: one penny in Davies' the grocer for a small plate of ham and a cracked egg, one penny for the Copenhagen Street flea pit on Saturday mornings, and one penny to take home to my mum. Happy memories!"

Another Eastender, Albert Mace, lived with his mum and a lodger in a big old house that belonged to the local church.

"The front door was made of solid oak. It must have been about four feet wide for it was big enough to push the wheel barrow through and out into the back yard where there was an upper workshop held up by four girders and we used to keep the goats, chickens and rabbits out there too.

"We used to load up the barrow with cycle parts and harnesses and then the lodger used to help me push the barrow all the way from Bethnal Green to The Cally. When we were all set up on the stones, I'd shout 'Penny a lump, valve rubber. Any lump for a penny!'"

Iris Tasker, still fairly local in Highbury, can remember trips to the market with her brothers. "On Tuesdays and Fridays, my brothers in turn, would hire a barrow for 6d (2½p) per day and take it by hand, with furniture and bric a brac, up to the Cally.

"It was a marvellous atmosphere there, and I was supposed to be going to school, but I remember being allowed to help my brother (who was 10 years older than me). He told me to look after the stall while he went to have a sandwich and a cup of tea.

"Two ladies came looking at all the wares and picked up a lovely pair of Chinese coloured, leather shoes that had pointed toes, delicately turned up. They asked me how much the shoes were. My brother hadn't priced anything, so I said 'One shilling (5p)' They looked astonished, and repeated 'A shilling!' I thought that they were thinking that the shoes were too expensive, so I said 'Oh, alright — sixpence (2½p)!'

"They ran off very quickly after paying me, but I was very disappointed when my brother wasn't pleased with my sale! He was also furious when he found that I had also sold his tools . . . for 6d again!"

Such colourful tales. They all give us a peep into the life and times of the folk who frequented The Cally, but we cannot leave the scene of the market just yet without recalling one or two more stories . . . Perhaps they should be called cautionary tales?

Annie Secchi lives in Penn Road, Holloway these days, but as a child, she lived in North Road, literally on the market's back doorstep. She can recall, as a youngster, going across to the market at closing time with her friend Rosie Johnson, to search for beads which had fallen from the jewellery stalls. One day, she found more than she had bargained for — a box had been left behind by one of the stall holders. She peeped inside and saw a pair of men's leather shoes almost new. She picked them up thinking that her dad would be very pleased with her 'find', when suddenly, a voice shouted 'Oi! That's my box!' Annie argued and clutched the box tightly, but to no avail. The man who had shouted, rushed up and snatched the box away from her. "I can remember crying my eyes out over that incident!" recalls Annie.

In later years, Annie got a job at the wicker factory at the top of Market Road. The factory was converted from the Black Bull Hotel — one of the four original pubs that marked the boundary of the market square. It had since closed down as a pub though, following a particularly suspicious murder of one of the barmaids some years before. However, Annie, a fairly new girl, was conscientiously getting on with her job of making wicker baskets for 4711 Eau de Cologne bottles when she ran out of cane. She knew that fresh supplies were kept at the top of the building, so rather than ask for some, she decided to go and find some herself. As she mounted the stairs, a voice shrieked, "Don't go up there, Annie — there's a ghost upstairs!" Rumours abounded throughout the factory of sightings of a headless barmaid drifting through the top floor of the building. Annie flew downstairs like a scalded cat, and never went up again!

Before we leave the Black Bull, there is rather an eerie, psychic story to tell — Harriett Nicholas from Camden Town, a young girl given to uncanny dreams, was walking along York Way to the market with her brother one bright spring morning, when suddenly, her happy mood changed. She grabbed her brother's arm tightly and her face was transformed by fear. She pointed to the group of drovers advancing slowly towards them and she whispered hoarsely to her brother, "Cross the road! Quickly! Take me over the road! I'm not walking near that man! He's the murderer — I saw him in my dream!"

The noisy group of drovers were getting nearer and Harriett became more agitated, clutching her brother's arm with both hands now. "Quickly! Take me over the road!"

Her brother obliged, and the pair stood and watched the band of cussing, complaining men pass by on the other side. When they were further away, Harriett calmed down a little. She explained to her brother that she had had a vivid dream the previous night in which she had seen a brutal murder being committed. She didn't know how, or who, or where, but at the very thought of the dream, she shivered involuntarily.

So who was the drover? Was he the one who had murdered the barmaid in the Black Bull? Harriett couldn't say.

A spine-chilling tale, this one, but nevertheless, true. It's a tale that has been handed down through Harriett's family, to her daughter, and told today by her grand-daughter, who has moved away from Camden Town these days, but still works in the area bordering on to the square mile of the old Caledonian Market.

Henry Mitchell of Kentish Town remembers the far off days when sheep used to graze on nearby Parliament Hill and cattle came down from Highgate to be driven to the market. One day, with a pal, he followed the cows to the slaughter house and stayed to watch a killing. He was not overjoyed by the sight, nor was his poor pal who turned a pale shade of green and promptly passed out on the spot! The poor fellow was escorted back home and was not able to eat anything for the rest of that day!

Henry recalls too, a day when he took his wife to The Cally to do some shopping. The unfortunate Mrs Mitchell, fascinated by the assortment of goods laid out on the cobbled stones, bent over to get a closer look, whereupon the elastic in her bloomers gave way. "I'll leave you to guess the rest of the story!" laughs Henry. "Luckily, I had a safety pin in my pocket that came to the rescue."

Mrs. Mitchell learned a lesson that day, and ever since, she's carried a safety pin everywhere with her in her purse!

What wonderful, warm-hearted stories there are, all recalled by folk who were there at the time — who can remember the way it was up at The Cally. Let the last tale go to Jane Brown whose fascination for the stones was recorded earlier. She wrote of her feelings about the market and set the scene for all these recollections spanning half a century, so it is only fitting that she should have the last word . . . thus we come full circle:

"A man called at my home one day while I was at the market. He said he had some goods he wished to sell hurriedly as he had some funeral expenses to meet. I got back after a bad day, having taken only twenty-five shillings (£1.25). Ten shillings (50p) of that had already gone on food so I told my mother I couldn't speculate with the only fifteen shillings (75p) I had left.

"The man called again next morning and he was so insistent that I finally went with him to see the things he had. I turned the first thing down at once. It was a brass bedstead and I should have needed a van to get it to market. He then bought out some oddments of china. They were not very good, but I thought they might go if they were priced cheaply so I offered him five shillings. With only ten shillings left, and more by way of preparing to gc than as meaning him to find anything else, I said, 'There is nothing else, I suppose?'

"'Yes. My wife had a mania for collecting brass chains. She has just died you know.' He fetched a box and showed me about ten chain necklaces and a number of bangles and

88

ear-rings. They would sell very easily, I thought, and risking a penniless weekend, I offered him my remaining ten shillings. He accepted, and I came away, wondering if I had been foolishly eager and thinking how glum a time lay ahead until I could go to The Cally again.

"When I got home, I naturally examined all the chains again, and I took a sudden breath. These were not brass chains. The bangles and ear-rings were not brass. They were all gold.

"The morality of dealing is that if you have bought an article and so far as you can judge, it was honestly come by in the first place, that article is yours. If it is worth less than you paid for it, no one but you will have to stand the loss. If it is worth more than either the seller or you thought at the time, it is equally yours. You may feel that special circumstances warrant you making a gesture, but it remains only a gesture from you.

"I took the jewellery to a local dealer and he gave me eighteen pounds for it. Eighteen pounds! It was wealth undreamed of! At home, there was only ten shillings worth of food — nothing else at all until I had been to the market again — and still nothing else if the weather was too bad to lay out my stuff. But I had eighteen pounds! I almost floated home.

"But then I felt that there were special circumstances in this case. The man was in trouble, bereft of his wife, and he had quite obviously been fond of her. He was also quite obviously in very poor circumstances or he would not have wanted to sell a few odds and ends which he regarded as worthless. I put nine pounds in an envelope and put it on one side to take round to him the next day.

"However, when I arrived at his rooms the next day, they were empty. The widower had packed up and left, and none of the neighbours could tell me where he had gone. Well, that was just his bad luck, I thought.

"But there is a sequel to the story. Some months later, I was buying a few goods from a local woman when she asked me,

'Do you remember poor old Sal?' but I didn't. The woman went on, 'But you bought some things from her husband after she died.' I had certainly not forgotten that. The woman continued, 'Sal was his wife. She was a prostitute and her husband had no idea of it. He thought the world of her to the last. And so that he shouldn't get suspicious about her having so much money, she used to put it into jewellery and then tell her husband it was brass. I never heard what came of it in the end, nor if he ever found out. It would have broken his heart if he had.'

"I said no more, but I did feel infinitely grateful that the man had gone by the time I got back with the nine pounds. It could have done no possible good to disillusion him at the last.

"'I heard the husband died a little while back' the woman was saying as she went away, 'but the local has never been the same since Sal's been gone.'

"It was a curious thought that the money which had been so much more than welcome to us at a time when we had needed it so badly, had indirectly come from the kind of traffic carried on by Sal. I could not help but think by what strange twists and quirks of Chance the affairs of we human beings are finally sorted out."

Chapter Ten

"You may sit down and examine the goods at your leisure . . . .
quite a pleasant occupation."

Those same quirks of chance and twists of fate often lead us mortals to travel on, up and away, to finally end up in far off lands, away from the homes of our childhood. There are many folk today who cherish early memories of The Cally, yet they are scattered widely around the world.

Shirley Darbyshire hailed from down under in Victoria, Australia. As a young journalist, she spent some time in England and wrote an account of her shopping trips in London for the Victoria Daily News. On the 22nd April 1930, the newspaper carried this article, written by Shirley Darbyshire:

"I have forsworn the West End of London as a shopping centre. The window displays lack interest and the conventiality is irksome. I now make my purchases further northward, for I find in the Caledonian Market, a richness and variety which should satisfy the most ardent seeker after adventure, for in The Cally, you never know what you may discover . . .

"The stallholders are as varied as their own goods. Some speak to you in the accents of Oxford, others reply in the broadest Cockney. Some women wear the flowing capes and wide brimmed hats popular in Chelsea. Others wear feathered hats and high heel boots and seem to have a dozen children to mind as well as their goods.

"The counter system does not prevail here. People spread their goods out all over the stones and you may sit down among them and examine them at your leisure — quite a pleasant occupation. I had a nasty shock when I looked over a display of antique jewellery. I happened to lean against the edge of the improvised counter and the whole thing slid playfully away from me. 'It's a pram, dearie,' said the befeathered proprietress, and sure enough, she had contrived a counter from planks of wood laid across the baby's pram. The dispossessed baby shared a place of honour with the dog beside a smoking brazier in the rear. The fact that neither of them were suffocated says much for the staying power of babies and dogs!

"Dusk descends early in Islington and over the hurly burly of visitors and vendors, naptha flares burn brightly and braziers of coal gleam through the shadows and send out a welcome warmth."

It was precisely that "welcome warmth" that made The Cally such an inviting market, and in recalling their long forgotten memories, people talking about it feel a warm glow of nostalgia in their hearts.

Stories come flooding in from far and wide. From West Cornwall, Connecticut in the United States, Michael Gannett writes:

"Yes, indeed. I remember London's Caledonian Market from when I first visited London in 1936 — lots of rubbish spread across the pavements with a few hidden pearls among the piles.

"No, I saw no diamond necklaces or Rembrandts which would have meant little to me then or since, but I did find for a great bargain, a complete set of uncancelled stamped envelopes issued on the occasion of Chicago's 1892 Exposition and a 1776 map of my home state of Connecticut, both of which items are still with me today.

"I returned to London many times after the War, but alas, there was no longer a Caledonian Market offering similar treasures or even diamond necklaces or Rembrandts."

Here, Michael mentions his frequent trips to London after the war, and his tinge of sadness at finding the Caledonian Market gone. Another strange but true tale is told by Fred White, a resident of the market area for many a long year.

One morning, not so very long ago, but a good 40 years since the days of the Cally, Fred was down on the platform at Caledonian Road underground station, waiting for a train to take him to work at The Bank of England in the City, when he chanced upon two 'Texas Cowboys' — complete with ten-gallon stetsons. As they walked towards him, they looked a little bemused and lost. Fred offered to help.

"Yessir," drawled one of the Yankee tourists. "We're looking for the Metropolitan Cattle Market. We think this is the right underground station?"

Fred had to smile. "Yes, you've got the right underground station," he said, "but I'm afraid you're about 40 years too late! The market was closed down just before the last war!"

"Well, you don't say!" said one of the Texans. "And we've heard all about that great market from the folks back home. They said 'Now you be sure to visit that Metropolitan Cattle Market while you're over in London Town.' We were looking forward to seeing some fine head of cattle, and now you tell us that the place is all done gone."

Fred glanced at his watch. He hadn't really got any time to spare, but he would have loved to have taken them around the site of the old market — to see the Clock Tower and the remains of the railings which enclosed the site where once a thousand cattle stood for auction.

"Look," said Fred. "If you go out of the station, turn right, and then right again at the traffic lights, and you'll find the Caledonian Park and the housing estates on the site of the old market. Have a look around and see what's left of a little bit of London's history."

Fred left the 'Cowboys' to go on their way as his train came in, and as the underground carried Fred along to work that morning, he closed his eyes and recalled some of his own happy childhood memories, when as a boy, he too rummaged over 'The Stones' for any leftovers, or watched the high-stepping horses jauntily pulling their gigs along Caledonian Road on a Friday night. He smiled as he thought of the two Americans coming over to look at the 'Cattle Auctions'. He could remember those days so well, and he could remember days when the whole of the market place was full of donkeys, brought over from Ireland . . .

94

Soon though, Fred's reverie was shattered as his train came in to the Bank Station, and he had another morning's work to attend to . . .

Joy Burton, from the Sunshine Coast in Queensland, Australia, remembers her very first signet ring:

"My dad splashed out and bought me a rolled gold signet ring for 4d (1½p)! I had it until it wore thin. It was on a stall of bankrupt jewellery, and I remember everyone saying we had got a bargain. Dad earned £2 a week as a kerb and gutter bricklayer, so money was not plentiful in our house.

"He also bought Mum a silver locket for 1/6d (7½p). I don't remember seeing any diamond necklaces, but I do remember the crowds pushing and shoving, the excitement of the place, and the pick-pockets too!

"We lived in Bognor Regis, but my relatives lived in Battersea, so when we went up to London, we'd go across to the Caledonian Market. My relatives had no spare bedrooms so when we stayed with them, we'd sleep in their beds at night, and when we got up, they'd go to bed! That could only happen in Cockney Land . . . Happy Days!"

Dennis Jackson grew up in Islington in the 'thirties. In later years, he married a Greek girl and finally settled in Limassol in Cyprus. These days, he spends much of his time reading, doing a little typing, but mostly, sitting on his balcony in the Cypriot sunshine, recalling warm memories of earlier years. From sunny Limassol come memories of 'Barmy Alf':

"I was born in Queens Head Street in 1925 so it was a considerable walk from there to the Old Caledonian Market, but us boys from the street often used to go there during the summer months, after we came home from school, but by about half past five, or six o'clock, the stallholders would be packing up.

"The stallholders would throw away all sorts of useful items because they couldn't be bothered to take them away, so a gang of us boys would set off from Queens Head Street, all pushing our home made carts or old prams and do the trek to the market. As we got to the bottom of North Road, the place was packed with people — all out to see what they could find. There was such a cross-section of people — the poor and the unemployed, pushing carts and barrows, rubbing shoulders with the well-dressed and the antique dealers who came in fine cars.

"I remember one stall which used to sell cigarette cards in sets and copies of old boys magazines like the Wizard, Hotspur, Rover and the Eagle. That was the stall that fascinated me most.

"I remember one particular evening when we were scrounging around, and one of my mates spotted a man arguing with a stallholder. He appeared to be trying to knock down the stallholder's price for some old First World War medals. 'Look! There's Barmy Alf!' said my mate.

"Now Barmy Alf lived in Queens Head Street, next door to me in fact. He had served in the army in India and also in the 1914-18 war. He really was 'barmy' and some of the things he did were quite outlandish, but he was harmless enough, and his antics gave us boys a good laugh! We stood watching him and eventually, he bought three medals.

"'So that's where he gets his medals — on the Caledonian front!' said my mate who had a book on medals. 'Do you know, I think he must have bought the Military Cross because only officers were awarded that.' Barmy Alf was very military in appearance with short, iron grey hair and a clipped moustache. We watched him buy his medals, then carried on with our hunting and forgot all about him.

"A couple of weeks later on a Friday evening when most of the occupants of Queens Head Street were in the pub, three of us boys were sitting on the wall when we saw Barmy Alf come out of The Old Queens Head, looking as though he had downed more than a few drinks. He swayed down to the house where he had lodgings and disappeared inside.

"Ten minutes later, he reappeared with the landlady's sheet wrapped around him, a turban on his head and clutching a three foot sabre. His face was covered in soot and he was wearing a pair of eastern slippers with turned-up toes. We watched idly, wondering what he was going to do.

"He took one look at us, then turned and roared, 'El Akbar!' He flew up the street to the corner and stood there waving the sabre around his head. 'Ha! Ha! Back you foreign devils! Take that! And that!' He made a stab at the wooden shutters of a shop. 'Have at you, you swine!' he shouted as he parried an imaginary foe. The three of us just stood there, doubled up with laughter. Then the landlady's husband came out of the pub. 'Cor blimey, it's Alf!' he shrieked. 'What are you doing?'

"At that, the pub cleared and everybody was out on the street, watching him and cheering him on. 'Go on Alf! Give it to 'em!'

"Three girls walked around the corner and were suddenly confronted by the apparition of a whirling dervish waving a lethal weapon at them. He leered at them with a devilish grin. The girls fled screaming towards Camden Passage with Alf chasing them and shouting 'Ha girls! Does your mother know you're out?'

"Eventually Barmy Alf was carried back home and sobered up. The turban was removed from his head, and the white sheet taken away for washing. Then the medals were removed from him as he was laid down on the bed. 'Where did you win the Military Cross, Alf?' someone asked.

"'Ah yes. That was given to me by my commanding officer for the part I played in the attack on Arras. They would have given me the Military Medal, but they ran out of those.' Everyone knew he was fibbing but nobody minded. His stories were too good and they gave everybody a laugh. But we boys knew where his medals had come from . . . and we didn't let on!"

A funny tale, and one that still gets a laugh when Dennis recounts it to his friends, nevertheless, it's true.

From Toronto in Canada comes the story of a fake fox fur from Joan Nash: "We bought my sister a fox fur cape which was the latest style in those days. My mother and I went on our own that day to pick it out. All my brothers and sisters had put some money in, and Mum and Dad said they would pay the balance. All together, we had about ten pounds — that was a lot of loot in those days!

"We hunted around all the stalls, looking at fox fur capes, but my sister had shown me the one that she fancied in a large store in Oxford Street. Eventually, we found one almost like it and we bartered for it, knocking the vendor down to nine pounds ten shillings! He even put it in a box for us and tied a beautiful ribbon round it. To this day, my sister still thinks we paid about fifty pounds for her fox fur!"

Again, all the way from Canada, come memories from Daphne Glenister who used to live in the newsagents and tobacconists shop at the corner of Hemingford and Lofting Road. Says Daphne, "My parents were always very busy with the business, so being an avid stamp collector, I often slipped out and away to The Cally where I browsed around the stalls, and often found a few rare stamps. My parents didn't like me visiting the market. Nowadays, I can see why!

"Another vivid memory is of Mr. Selwyn — the mounted policeman on a beautiful white horse. I took marzipan candies from the shop to feed to his horse as I went on my way up to the market!"

So many folk left England's green and pleasant land long ago to start a new life overseas. They took with them all their personal possessions and treasures from their homes so that they would have a reminder of their homeland. They also took with them their memories — of childhood, of their lives thus far, of London in general, and perhaps the old Caledonian Market in particular.

From Thornlie in Western Australia, Sidney Smith, a grand old veteran of 87 years, writes: "I remember my first visit to the Caledonian Market. It was during the first World War and I used to go along with my uncle to a small factory near the market where soap was made. It was a very small business, run by three men and one woman, and the product they made was called 'War Soap' — fitting for those times. The soap was sold in the market on Fridays, and I went with my uncle and the woman from the factory to sell it on one of the stalls. I always thought the market place was a cold, unprepossessing place with the hard cobble stones and cold iron pens.

"I remember another occasion, between the two wars, when I had arrived home on leave from the Army. My father invited me to go with him to an Auction Room and pick up some items to sell in the market. When we arrived at The Cally, dad laid out a cloth on the cobble stones and set up the things he had to sell — nothing really of great value.

"However, he did have a rather nice statue which two elderly ladies took a fancy to. They asked 'How much?' When dad told them the price, they made a lower offer, but dad turned it down and the two ladies walked away. I pointed out to dad that he should have let them have it because of the crack along the side. 'Did it have a crack in it?' asked dad, turning it over in his hands. 'Why didn't you tell me before!'

"I spent the rest of the day wandering around the stalls, looking for anything interesting. I was amazed at the number of dealers there were, all using magnifying glasses to examine trinkets that must have had a certain value. Looking back over the years now, I still remember that feeling of coldness that somehow got into my very bones there, but for all that, I don't like to see old London landmarks having to make way for more modern buildings . . ."

An even more senior citizen, George Sleigh, hailing from Ontario in Canada, left England more than 77 years ago — in 1912 in fact. In a beautifully neat hand for his advancing years, George writes: "Yes — I remember the market, we called it 'The Stones'. I used to rummage around there for hours, searching happily. What for? You never knew what you were looking for until you found it! I loved rooting around the old book stalls. I was very young in those days, and apprenticed as a compositor to Eyre and Spottiswood, His Majesty's Printers. We set the type up all by hand on a stick in those days. I've been away from England for a long, long while now, but I still dream of home — 'my country, right or wrong'.

"I remember so vividly the fascinating beauty of the pink May trees in the London parks in the spring. All my memories of London are as warm as the sun on a red brick wall."

The last tale that comes from overseas is told by Estelle Henri of her Uncle Max who hails from Israel now. Estelle spends half of her time at home in Essex and the other half in Israel with other members of the family. She recalls this tale which is often told at family gatherings, sometimes as a caution to the younger ones as much as for amusement:

"My grandmother, Sadie Isaacs, as a young woman, had a housewares stall in the Caledonian Market in the 'twenties. The outstanding memory of that era was an incident which bought a sense of shame and rage to grandmother, but in later years, members of the family recounted the tale as an amusing anecdote — even if there was a moral in it somewhere!

"One of Gran's sons, Uncle Max, was apparently up to no good in the market one day for he was very promptly marched before the juvenile court which sat nearby in the Vernon Chapel, Vernon Square. (This was in May, 1929, when Uncle Max was aged fourteen years).

"Max was found guilty of some thoroughly disgraceful offence and he was sentenced to be birched. Normally, the flogging took place at a police station, but on this particular day, a great police review was about to take place in Hyde Park in connection with the Police Centenary. The police were therefore making all their preparations for the occasion and were much too busy to deal with such mundane entities as the birching of wayward boys.

"Justice was instantaneous in those days and it was therefore decided that the punishment should take place there and then in Vernon Chapel itself. Three or four hefty gentlemen were engaged as custodians for the crestfallen Max, and then a doctor was sought to ascertain Max's fitness and to oversee the subsequent proceedings.

"Eventually, a lady doctor from the Board of Education, a certain Miss Bywaters, was found to be available, and thereupon, Max was required to strip to the buff to undergo a medical scrutiny. (This scrutiny consisted mainly of having to stand on tiptoe and cough rather loudly a few times — or so Max later confided to his brother.)

"Grandmother, a hardworking widow, was outraged by the shame thus brought upon the family, and she demanded that she be allowed to administer the thrashing herself. This demand was granted since the law allowed that a parent or guardian could execute the punishment. This however, did NOT spare the rod for Uncle Max, for grandmother was then still in her thirties, and built like a navvy! Thus, Uncle Max, still in his birthday suit, touched his toes and came on the receiving end of Gran's rude justice which brought a certain blush to his cheeks!

"My father often reflected that there cannot have been many persons, apart perhaps from some orders of nunnery taking their vows, who have appeared naked, by order, in a chapel. He said it was a kind of rebirth for Uncle Max!"

Estelle often wondered why the family always referred to Uncle Max as "Blossie", but in later years, the secret of his nickname was revealed to her: apparently, the German Jewish lady from whom Uncle Max had stolen, was also present in Vernon Chapel on that fateful day. She referred to Max as 'Bloss' (German for nude) as a result of his sojourn in the altogether! Poor Max Isaacs, now living in Israel, has never been able to live it down, but even so, he's tickled pink today to learn that he has become 'a little bit of social history!'

Such stories from all over the world give us just a brief glimpse into this corner of London where crowds thronged and mingled, to sell, stare and steal, to bargain, banter and buy. It's a corner that demanded one's attention. It was fascinating, vibrant and bewildering, yet it couldn't be ignored.

Nowadays, the hubbub has died away and the stalls have moved on into that grand market in the sky. Even 'The Stones' have long since disappeared beneath a grassy carpet, but still the stories linger on . . .

Chapter Eleven

The market clock stood, regularly chiming the hours for those who lived nearby and experiencing its own finest hour at 10.00 on Friday mornings

The stories linger but time marches resolutely on. Days and weeks, months and years tick relentlessly by, but the Market Clock remains, guarding its ghosts and its memories. It's a testimony of a bygone era. A monument to a time when it was all important, rising majestically over the turmoil beneath, chiming the hours with a ring of defiance.

But alas, it no longer marks the passing of time. Still standing gracefully, although a little the worse for wear, London's largest turret clock is feeling the weight of its one hundred and thirty five years, and the necessary money required to effect the costly repairs has all but run out. So the Market Clock no longer chimes the hours or ticks off the passing minutes. Instead, it stands peacefully, even if somewhat incongruously, in a grassy park amid a modern housing estate. But at least it stands.

The very first foundation stone for the clock was laid in March 1854 and its inscription reads:

METROPOLITAN CATTLE MARKET
The Rt. Hon. Thomas Sydney, Lord Mayor
First stone of the Clock Tower laid in the Seventeenth Year
of the reign of Queen Victoria by
Henry Lowman Taylor Esq.,
The Chairman of the Committee
whose names surround the City Arms.
March 24th, 1854.

The turret clock at a height of 160 feet, became one of London's most well known landmarks, situated as it was on the high ground of Islington, commanding a view over the spires of the City to the river and beyond to the Surrey Hills, and away to the rolling plains of Hertfordshire and Middlesex in the north.

Thus it stood, regularly chiming the hours for those who lived nearby and experiencing its own finest hour at 10.00 on Friday mornings! But in 1940, catastrophe struck.

A landmine devastated that area between Hungerford Road and North Road facing York Way, and the clock, shaken to its very foundations, ticked no more. It's hands stopped abruptly at 9.15 pm and for the next thirteen years, it remained silent until somebody could be found to do the necessary repairs.

At length, Mrs Hilda Buggins of Thwaites and Reeds in Bowling Green Lane, clockmakers extraordinaire for 276 years, came to the rescue. Mrs Buggins had been running the firm for many years since the death of her husband, the late great grandson of the Mr Buggins who had bought the business in 1740 — when there was still a bowling green in the lane.

Many fragments of the original glass had to be chipped out and replaced. The structure was newly glazed with opal ware and double backed with plate glass to protect it from the wind. These major works took three months to carry out. Finally, on 23rd January 1953, everything was ready. Mr. Embury of Thwaites and Reeds, who had done much of the repair work under Hilda Buggins' supervision, stood at the top of the clocktower, and turned the massive handle. At three o'clock that afternoon, the Market Clock chimed once more.

Since that day, Jim Burrows has been the official nursemaid and Guardian of The Clock. A former Corporation of London employee and engineer in the slaughterhouses, Jim has known and loved 'his' clock since childhood. Born virtually in its shadow in Cliff Villas, Jimmy played in the market with all the other local lads, running for pitches, helping stallholders to load and unload and generally earning the odd copper here and there. He went to Brecknock and Hungerford schools, then in mid 1947, went to serve his King and Country with the British Army in the Far East.

On being demobbed in 1952, Jim arrived home on the troop ship Dunera and settled down to enjoy his extended leave. Then he took a job as an engineer for the Corporation of London, and part of his duties included looking after the

Market Clock. This meant winding up the mechanism once a week, by hand, to ensure that the bells chimed at exactly the right moment, and to see that every little cog, nut and wheel was well greased and running smoothly.

It wasn't long before this tall, elegant white lady cast her spell upon Jim, causing him to spend long hours with her until he was passionately in love. So eager was he to caress her mechanism and oil her working parts, that he never noticed how quickly time passed when in her company! His passion grew into a life-long love affair, so much so that when the Corporation moved Jim into a new flat in Kinefold House, he chose the flat whose bedroom window was immediately opposite his clock's western face!

The Market Clock, together with the slaughter houses, were inspected regularly by the Court of Common Council. One of the Council members, knowing Jim was an engineer, introduced him to a colleague who needed a little emergency job done on a converted transport bus — thus, Jim met Dick Whittington who was slowly but surely on his way to securing a 'decent' job with the Corporation, following in the footsteps of his famous ancestor (and his cat).

Jim and Dick became firm friends while working on the transport bus together and their friendship continued when Dick actually became the Lord Chamberlain and inhabited London's Guildhall.

As it happened, one day, not so long ago, a smart American executive type came wandering around Caledonian Park. He was taking photographs of the Market Clock and expressing great interest in it from all angles. A group of youngsters, playing football in the park, kept a keen eye on this stranger and his antics.

"Hi kids! Who owns this clock, d'ya know?" The youngsters, sensing some adventure here, led the American to Jim Burrows' flat in Kinefold House. Jim got the shock of his life when the American asked how much he wanted for his 'white elephant'!

"It's not mine!" he protested. "It's not for sale! I'm only the caretaker!" The American however, was very persistent, so Jim offered him a trip to the top of the tower to enjoy the view. Greatly impressed, the American doubled his price and even offered to take Jim, and his whole family, to America too, so that the clock could be kept in pristine condition and good working order!

From the balcony of the clock, Jim pointed down to Pentonville prison. "Look, Yank," said Jim. "This clock is not for sale. It's not mine, and if I listen to you and your offers, I'll end up inside there!"

The guided tour of the Market Clock ended with a trip to the White Horse where old framed photographs of Caledonian Market life grace almost every wall. "Drinks all round!" said the American executive, and everybody cheered.

Meanwhile, the American explained to Jim that he really was part of a consortium who were seeking to buy some old London buildings with which to adorn the beautiful Lake Havasu in Arizona.

"I'll tell you what you can do, Yank," said Jim. "You go down to the Guildhall and see the Lord Chamberlain. His name is Dick Whittington and he's a friend of mine. Tell him I sent you, and ask him if he's got an old building or two to flog you!"

A few weeks later, Jim met up with his pal, Dick. "Hey, Jim," said Dick. "Did you meet some nice American people recently?"

"Yes — I did," Jim replied. "Some smart guy who wanted to buy my clock. He offered me a fortune! I took him up the Clock Tower, then we had a drink and got a bit happy, so I sent him out of the pub to go and see you. Sorry!"

"No, Jim," said Dick. I sent him up to see YOU! He's part of some money-making company that wants to buy up old buildings in London. I thought you might have been able to negotiate for him. You see, I am 'flogging' him, as you so nicely put it, our old London Bridge because we haven't got any more use for it! We're getting a new and wider one."

"Well, I'll be damned!" said Jim.

"Yes — what a joke! They're shipping it over to America in bits and they're going to rebuild it over a lake in the Arizona desert. The funniest part is — they think it's Tower Bridge!"

This story found its way into the hands of an advertising agency who duly passed it on to a well-known lager company. Maybe it sounds familiar to you . . .

Jim Burrows of course, can tell many more tales about his clock which span his thirty five years as the official time keeper, but his love for the Market Clock and his dedication to keeping it in good shape are plain to see. Many and long are the hours and much of his own money has been spent in keeping the clock in trim. Jim would love to see the Market Clock restored to its former glory, with strengthened glass bricks replacing the broken panes and the clock face cleaned of graffiti. He has visions of the inside being cleaned of muck and debris with safe stairways leading up to one of the finest views in London, and perhaps giving guided tours to tourists.

His dearest wish is for the clock to be floodlit by night for all to see. It wouldn't be a difficult job and Jim, the engineer, could cope with it easily. There it would stand, illuminated, as a memorial to the days of the Old Caledonian Market, and to a man who loved and cared for a clock. As Jim says, "We make our own memorials. Who wants paper fame?"

*   *   *

In 1939, there was one question on everybody's lips that dominated market conversation. "Will there be a war? What will happen to the market?" There was an ominous atmosphere that hung like a heavy rain cloud over the stones.

Eventually, the sirens did begin to sound. People lived in fear and anxiety and did not congregate in large crowds any more. The market folk, who had outlived one world war, prepared to do battle with another one, but it was not to be. The last market day was held in August 1939. As the stall holders packed up their wares for the last time, they did so with heavy hearts. People purposely lingered long in the gathering dusk, savouring the last moments before nightfall, reluctant to go their homes, perhaps never to come back again. "Let's just have one more drink in The Lamb before we go . . ."

With the twilight came the kids, scampering across the stones and through the empty stalls, looking for some last bits of 'treasure' to take home, knowing that there wouldn't be any more opportunities to go hunting again for a little while . . .

At the outbreak of war, the open space was requisitioned by the Army to be used as a storage depot for goods and vehicles. Later, the Post Office also took over part of the site as a maintenance garage for their red Royal Mail vans.

It was not long before tufts of grass began to grow between the cobbles and cracks appeared in the glass panes of the banking house windows. The whole area lay empty and desolate, waiting for the cheery return of the thronging crowd of marketeers.

After the war, London slowly returned to sanity once more. People began to pick up the pieces and return to their 'normal' lives again. The Caledonian Market stallholders collected together some of the goods which had been locked away for several years and waited for the market to re-open. And waited.

By 1949, the Corporation of London showed no signs of opening up the gates at 10.00 am on a Friday again although the Army had left the site three years previously. Something had to be done to get the Corporation moving.

Jane Brown took the initiative. In August 1949, together with her husband Don, she contacted about 80 former stallholders and invited them to an Open Meeting in a church hall in the West End. The hall was packed with people, all delighted to see one another again after such a long interval. "Fancy meeting you again!" was the standard remark of the evening. Everybody vociferously supported the re-opening of The Cally. Their livelihood depended on it.

During the evening, the Caledonian Market Traders Association was formed. Don Brown was elected Secretary and Jane was voted Chairman. A six point campaign policy was adopted unanimously. The case for re-opening the market was based on the fact that it had the potential to become a dollar earner, as it had been previously with the patronage of the American tourists to London.

The first step of the campaign would be to examine the charter granted by Henry II to establish and investigate the rights of market traders. Secondly, a petition was to be drawn up and taken to the Lord Mayor and Parliament, or failing that, the King himself.

Feeling ran high on the subject and the meeting was a rowdy one. Said Mrs Romaine, who had kept a stall at The Cally since 1914: "There are dozens of us who have stuff put away which has not seen the light of day since the market closed. If those goods were put up on the stalls again, I'm sure many people would come along and make a deal with us. It would benefit the poor as well as ourselves."

Bill Bland, Islington born and bred, whose mother was in the market for 60 years, had memories of The Cally himself since the age of four. "The market could be opened again at the cost of about four gate-men, six ticket collectors, and a few cans of whitewash to mark out the pitches," he said. "It would be a case of £100 against the £14 million proposed for the Festival of Britain. And we can sell anything there — things you can't possibly get anywhere else."

When the market closed in 1939, many stallholders had already paid a month's rent in advance. They were told that they could have their money returned, or leave it there as a stall reservation for the eventual re-opening.

Jane Brown was very positive that the campaign would get official backing. "My one idea in life is to get that market opened again," she told an Islington Gazette reporter, forty years ago.

Eighty year old Frank Prattley, whose grandfather had kept a market stall, summed up the feeling of the traders by saying, "If it's the last thing I do, I'll push my barrow up to the market again."

Sadly, Frank never got his wish for even with 13,500 signatures on their petition, the Caledonian Market Traders Association were not successful with their campaign. Permission to return to the market was not granted by the Court of Common Council. Instead, the 13,500 petitioners were offered a New Caledonian Market site in Bermondsey, at the junction of Bermondsey Street and Tower Bridge Road. In 1950, the film star Valerie Hobson opened the new market and some 200 stalls began to ply their trade in antiques, bric a brac and curios on a Friday.

It didn't take long for the name 'New Caledonian Market' to die out though. Neither did it take very long for 'Bermondsey Market' to establish itself as purely an antique market. These days, it is the professional dealers and experts in their own special lines who set up very early in the morning — before dawn in fact — to do a brisk trade in antiques and curios, mostly to the American tourists who rise early in order to do it all and see it all.

Bermondsey Market is a far cry from the days of The Cally though for somehow, the old fashioned community and kindred spirit is no longer there. You do not have to clamour at the gates or fight for a pitch at Bermondsey, nor can you find anything from a pin to an elephant at the stalls there — but perhaps you don't even want to. There is a certain curiosity there though, and no doubt many a bargain too, if you know what you are looking for.

But the intimacy and the debauchery of The Cally do not live on at Bermondsey. Gone is the sheer excitement of wandering through a motley collection of market stalls, not knowing what could possibly be unearthed beneath Aunt Gladys's flowing feather boa or the broken picture frame . . . That was enough in itself to make the very adrenalin flow, not to mention the haggling, the bartering or even the standing back to watch somebody else make a spectacle of themselves. Gone too is the profligacy of the Cally's countless infamous characters and gone is the spirit and the warmth of another age.

There never was another market like the Old Caledonian and there will never be another one like it again . . .

*   *   *

And what of the old Caledonian Market site today?

Until 1953, the slaughter houses were still in operation and the cows came from the railway sidings in Piper Close to march slowly up North Road to their fate. Then the London County Council, in their wisdom, decided that the abattoirs were not hygienic any more, thus they were closed down. Having disposed of the last vestiges of the Cally to Bermondsey, it was considered that the whole site could now be put to much better use as a housing area for council homes were desperately needed in Islington, so in 1965, the building began.

The Corporation of London today owns Kinefold, Lambfold, Penfields and Shepherd Houses, all of which were completed in 1968. Islington Borough Council owns Kerry, Tamworth,

112

Southdown and Clocktower Place, all collectively known as the Market Estate, and providing homes for some 700 tenants. In 1975, the sheltered housing accommodation of Hawberry House was built and together with the Drovers Day Centre for the elderly and infirm, the Goodinge Health Centre and the St. Francis Church Centre, the picture was completed.

The Clock Tower forms the focal point for the whole of the housing development and the Caledonian Park provides the green open space for recreation. Underneath the grassy park lie the same old blue cobbled stones that once echoed to the sound of a million footsteps. The same old iron railings that once bore the proud animal heads marking the boundary of the market, still line the perimeter of Caledonian Park.

On the other side of Market Road, the two Astroturfs replace the animal lairs and the water fountain, although at the far side of the pitches, the original arched wall of the lairs can still be seen, as can just a couple of the old iron rings to which the animals were once tethered.

The Black Bull disappeared in flames sometime in the late 'thirties, but the Lion, the Lamb and the White Horse continue to ply their trade to local residents. Maybe the thirsty ghosts of stallholders and market folk wander through the bars at night waiting for opening time. Perhaps they are even waiting for the market itself to open once more. Who knows? The three pubs are just a little the worse for wear these days but they had their moments in days gone by.

Those days are gone now — into the annals of history, and buried with them is a part of London's street life, as rich in colour, folklore and legend as any historical pageant.

Many of the folk mentioned in this book have passed on now to another time and another place but there are many more who perhaps on reading this collection of tales, will suddenly recall from the back of their mind, their own personal memories of The Cally. Perchance they too will wax lyrical and say, "Oh yes! I remember when . . .!"

August 1989 marks the 50th anniversary of the grand old days of The Cally. By the turn of the century, there may still be a few folk who will be able to recall the last market day before the war. After that, the old Caledonian Market will be a closed book, but perhaps these few tales will live on and recall the stories of the 'greatest market in the world' for posterity; if they do, that will be good enough for me.

Postscript

As for me — what do I remember? Unfortunately, I'm too young to remember any of those wonderful days. As a child, I remember seeing the cows being driven up North Road and complaining noisily all the way .... Whilst out walking with my mother one day, along Hilmarton Road, we turned the corner into Caledonian Road and came face to face with the cows. My mother screamed, and we both ran!

From Hungerford School, I often walked home 'the back way' via the 'rec' and if time permitted, I'd squeeze through the railings with my brother to play on the cobble stones for a while . . . And many were the nights when sleep eluded me and I lay in bed, waiting to hear the comforting chimes of the Old Market Clock . . .

A few years ago, a local history project led by a teacher at Hungerford Infants School, renewed my interest in the Old Caledonian Market. I began to collect stories of the market, just for fun — and for my own personal interest as I had always lived in the area and had an interest in local history. Little did I know how engrossed I would become in the tales told to me by many wonderful old folk who loved to talk about themselves and their past. The pictures painted for me by their words made me feel as though I actually knew the characters almost as well as they did. I began to feel the atmosphere of Friday Market and I even began to wonder if I might perhaps have been there in another life!

This collection of market reminiscences really only touches the surface. There are many more tales which abound in the minds of people today — people scattered far and wide. Perhaps you've read this book and can recall from the back of your mind, a story you know, or something that happened to you. Perhaps you even have a tale to tell?

Sadly, I've had to leave out a multitude of stories for they arrived too late for this book. Letters still land on my desk from New Zealand, Canada, The States and other assorted places. There may well be enough for another collection of market tales. Volume two? Then we'll all have a chance to go Up The Cally Again!

MARJORIE EDWARDS

Bibliography

Smithfield Past and Present by A. Forshaw and T. Bergstrom, 1980

London Recollected, Volume II by Walter Thornbury

Islington Industrial Exhibition 1923, Handbook and Exhibition Guide

Streets with a Story by Eric A. Willatts, 1987

I had a Pitch on the Stones by Jane Brown, 1949

Illustrated London News, various editions, 1855

Leisure Hour Magazine, 1855 and 1856

London Markets by W.J. Passingham, 1935

Islington Local History Library

The Library of the Corporation of London at The Guildhall

British Newspaper Library at Hendon

Islington Gazette Archives

Victoria Daily News, Australia 1930

£3·99.